THE POE

ADAPTED FOR THE CONTEMPORARY READER BY
JAMES HARRIS

ISBN: 9781797526218

COPYRIGHT © 2019 JAMES HARRIS
ALL RIGHTS RESERVED

TABLE OF CONTENTS

POEM 1 THE OBSTRUCTION OF CID 4

POEM 2 THE MARRIAGE OF CID'S DAUGHTERS 50

POEM 3 THE WOOD OF CORPES 100

POEM 1

THE OBSTRUCTION OF CID

He turned and looked at them, cried and was very sore,
As he saw the open gate and the locks broken off the door,
And the pegs of the jacket, or coat where no longer hung,
No hawk was there perched, and no falcon's notes were sung.
My God Cid sighed so deeply, the pain that was in his heart,
And he spoke so well and wisely: "You in Heaven are my chart,
Our Father and our Master, now I give thanks to You.
Through their wickedness my enemies have attacked me out the blue."

Then they shook the reins, heeled the horse to ride afar.
They had the crow on their right hand, which was Cid's from Vivar;
And as they entered Burgos, on their left it led.
Cid shrugged his shoulders, and Cid shook his head:
"Good news from Alvar Fanez, we are banished with a seal,
But on a day with honour, will we find ourselves in Castile.

Cid Roy Diaz entered Burgos, with sixty men thick,
And to look at him, the men and women ran so quick.
And with their wives at the windows the townsmen stood close by,
And they cried in sorrow, their grief had risen high.
As with one mouth, together they spoke with one accord:
"God, what a noble man, and he is a worthy Lord."

They would have made him welcome, but none dared do the thing,
Due to their fear of Don Alfonso, and the fury of the King.
His order for Burgos didn't arrive, until the evening fell,
With utmost care they brought it, and it was sealed as well,
'That no man give Roy Diaz shelter, seriously to take heed,
And if someone gave him shelter, to let him know indeed.

He will lose his whole house, actually, the eyes within his head,
Nothing left, not his soul or body, will be found instead.
The Christians had great sorrow, and from his face they hid.
Because none dared to speak to, or say a word to Cid.
Then the messenger left, and went to his home, heading straight.
But when he got there, they had locked and blocked the gate.

Their fear of King Alfonso, had inspired them to do so,
But Cid did not force his entrance, to avoid any cut or blow.
They did not dare to open, so his men loudly gave the call,
But nothing was said in answer from the men within the hall.
My God Cid drove onward, to the doorway did he go.
He removed his foot from the stirrup, and struck the door one blow.
Yet the door would not open, because they had barred it fast.
But a lady of the chambers, came to him at last:

"Outstanding warrior in a fine time you hold the sword.
'This is the King's will. Last night came the mandate of our Lord.
With utmost care they brought it, and it was sealed with care:

None would dare to greet you, not for any cause they dare.
And if we do, we forfeit houses and lands instead.
Actually we will lose, moreover, the eyes within the head
And Cid, with our misfortune, nothing you will gain.
May God help you with all his power and support you in your pain."

And so this she spoke, and then she left for home.
Cid saw he lacked the King's favor and had to do this on his own.
He left the door; and onward he went, throughout Burgos town.
Until he had reached Saint Mary's, and then he swiftly got down

He fell on his knees and prayed, with a true heart of force,
and when the prayer were over, he mounted on the horse.
North from the gate and over Arlanzon he went.
There on the sand by Burgos, Cid put up his tent.
Roy Diaz, who was un-favoured and barred from the King's land,
Because no one would greet him, camped alone there on the sand.
With a fine group of men, camping as if within the wood.
No one would let him into Burgos, to buy any food if he could.
No food for a day, they did not dare to sell,
However, Good Martin Antolinez was in Burgos as well.
To Cid and his men, much wine and bread he came to give,
That he had bought with him, he said I will ensure you live.

The great warrior was content, and his men were of good cheer,
Martin Antolinez spoke, and his counsel you will hear:
"In happy hour, Cid, most surely you were born,

But we are on the edge of danger, and the following I will warn.
Tonight let us stay here, but in the morning we must run,

Because someone will condemn me, for the service I have done.
Sooner or later, as I escape, the King will search the earth,
For friendship's sake; if not, my wealth, there is nothing it is worth.

Then Cid said, who had wrapped himself in steel:
"Oh Martin Antolinez, you're loyal and possess good zeal.
And if I live, from now on I will pay you double rent,
But all my silver is gone, and all my gold I have almost spent.
And you see well enough that there's none I bring with me,
And I am in need of much, for my good company.
Since by chance I win nothing, by my might then I must make.
I desire, due to your counsel, to fill boxes for you to take.

With the sand we will fill them, as if they were funded,
And cover them with embossed leather and nails well studded.

The leather will be reddish, and well gilded every nail.
On my behalf please rush, to Vidas and Raquel.
Since in Burgos they forbid me to purchase any thing,
And the King withdrew his favor, to them my goods I can't bring.
They are heavy, and I must pawn them for whatever's right.
And so the Christians may not see it, you must go by night.
May the Creator judge it, and all the Saints be the choir,
I can do no more, and I do that against my desire.
"Martin did not stay, through Burgos he rushed, and then he

came,
To the Castle of Vidas and Raquel, and demanded them by name.

Raquel and Vidas sat to count their goods and profits through,
When Antolinez came, what a prudent man so true.
"Raquel and Vidas, am I not dear to your heart,
I would like to confide in you." All three then went apart.

"Give me your hands Raquel and Vidas, and please be sure,
That you will not betray me to Christian or to Moor.
I will make you rich forever. You will need never need,
When he went to gather the taxes the Champion and better breed,
Gathered many rich goods, and only kept the best.
Therefore this accusation against him was addressed.
And now two mighty boxes full of pure gold, he holds.
Why he lost the King's favor any man can notice when he beholds.
He has left his halls and houses, his meadow and his field,
And the boxes he cannot bring to you or he will be revealed.
The Champion wants to deliver the boxes to your trust.
And that you lend him what you think is just.
You take the boxes and keep them, but swear a great oath here,
That you will not look within them for the space of all this year."

The two discussed the offer: "Something for our profit we must endure,
In all transactions. He gained something in the country of the Moor,
When he went there, many goods he brought away,

But the one who is bared from the city, brings us gold to pay.
Let us together take the two boxes of gold,
And put them in some place where they will be unseen while we hold.

"What the Lord Cid demanded, please let us hear,
And what will be our lending for the space of all this year?"
Martin Antolinez said like a prudent man and true:
"Whatever you deem right and just, Cid desires it of you.
He will ask for little, since his goods are left in a safe place.
But men on all sides beg Cid for his grace.
Six hundred, will stand him in good stead ."
"We will give it to him gladly," Raquel and Vidas said.

"'Right now Cid is having trouble, so I should take the money there,
Raquel and Vidas answered: "This is not how to settle the affair.
Prudent men first take their deposit and after give the fee."

Martin Antolinez said: "So be it as for me.
Come to the great Champion as this is just and fair,
Then we will help you with the chests, and put them in your care,
And to do this in secret, no Moor or Christian will hear the tale."

"We are quite content with that, " said Vidas and Raquel,

"You will have six hundred when the chests are with us. "
They and Martin Antolinez rode away swiftly kicking up the dust.

They were exceedingly glad. Over the bridge he did not go,
But through the stream, which no other Burgalese man would know,
Finally, they observed the Champion's tent.
When they entered to kiss his hands they bent.
My Lord Cid smiled at them and to them he said:
"Ah, Don Raquel and Vidas, I thought you had forgotten me instead!
And now I must avoid who has banished me in disgrace,
As the king from me in anger has turned away his face.
I deem that from my earnings you will gain somewhat of worth.
And you will lack nothing while you dwell upon the earth.'
A-kissing of his hands immediately to Raquel and Vidas fell.
Good Martin Antolinez had made the bargain well,
That for the chests, six hundred they will lend,
And keep the chests safe, until the year has made an end.
So their word was given and sworn to him once more,
If they looked within them, that the deal would be done for,
Cid would never give them one grain of pay.
Martin said, "Let the chests be taken as swiftly as they may,
Take them, Raquel and Vidas, and keep the bees from the honey.
And we will go with you for the money,
Here, when the first cock crows my Lord Cid must depart."
At the loading of the chests you could see the great joy within the heart.
Because they could not lift the chests up, although fit and healthy,
To Vidas and Raquel – the chests would make them wealthy.
And they would be rich forever until their two lives came to an end,
The hand of my good Lord Cid, Raquel had kissed again:

"Ha! Champion, it went exactly as you planned,
From Castile you go to the men of a strange land.

Good fortune and great your gain will be,
Ah Cid, I kiss your hands again -- but please make a gift to me

Bring me a Moorish jacket splendidly knit in red. "

"So be it. It is granted," Cid then said,

"If from abroad I bring it, well does the matter stand;
If not, take it from the boxes I leave here in your hand. "

And then Raquel and Vidas took the two chests away.
With Martin Antolinez into Burgos without delay.
And with great care, and caution to their dwelling sped.
And in the middle of the hall a braided quilt they spread.
And a milk-white cloth of linen on top they did unfold.
Three hundred coins of silver in front of them, for Martin to hold.
Martin took them, and the coins he weighed,
And then for the other coins, three hundred in gold they paid.
Martin had five aides, he loaded each, as the coins weighed a tonne.
You will hear what Don Martin said when all of this was done:

"Ha! Don Raquel and Vidas, you have the chests, the two.
Well I deserve a reward, for obtaining this prize for you."

Vidas and Raquel stepped forward, "We will pay a sum:
And give a fair present for our profit you have won.
Good Martin Antolinez in Burgos where you dwell,

We will give a present which you deserve so well.
Get yourself some trousers and a rich coat for outdoors.
You have earned it, for a present these thirty coins are yours.
Because it's fair and honest, in our favour you will stand
Our part of this bargain to which we gave our hand "

Don Martin thanked them, took the coins and then withdrew,
But before he left the dwelling he wished well to the two.
He went out from Burgos, over the Arlanzon he went.
And him who in good hour was born he found within his tent.
Cid arose and welcomed him, with arms held wide and far:

"You are welcome Antolinez, my good friend that you are!
May you live until the season when you reap some gain from me."

"Here I have come, my Champion, with as good intentions as might be.
You have won six hundred, and thirty more have I.
Quickly order that they pack the tents and let us swiftly fly.
In San Pedro de Cardenas let us hear the cock crow away,
We will see your prudent lady, but short will be our stay.
It is necessary for us to go from the kingdom to over there,
Because the season of our suffering slowly ends while we bear."

They spoke these words and straight away the tents were stowed,
Lord Cid rode so swiftly with his men upon the road.
And on to Saint Mary's the horse's head he steered,
And with his right hand crossed himself: "God, I thank you, the revered.

Heaven and Earth that rules, let your favour grace me.
Directly I must go to Castile, Holy Saint Mary please take me.
Because I look at the King with anger, I don't know how many times,
I will live there for my life, but may your grace watch over from the skies.
Blessed Virgin, guard me night and day.
If you do so and good fortune comes my way,
I will offer such gratitude at the altar, and I swear
Most sincerely that I will give a thousand sermons there."

And the Lord Cid departed, as well as a good man may,
Without delay they rode the horses, and out they dashed away.
Good Martin Antolinez said, in Burgos where they dwell:

"I would see my lady gladly and advise my people well,
From now on, it doesn't bother me what they do,
Even if the King took it all, like the sunrise I will come to you."

Martin went back to Burgos but my Lord Cid wasn't done.
To San Pedro of Cardena as hard as his horse could run,
With all his men around him who served him as his wing,
And it was close to morning, so the birds began to sing.
When at last my Lord the Champion to San Pedro had came,
God's Christian the Abbot, Don Sancho was his name,
And he was saying prayers at the ringing of a bell.
With five good ladies in waiting Jimena was there as well.
They prayed to Saint Peter, God and to the son:
"O you who guide all mankind, support the Champion."

One knocked at the doorway, to hear the news told then.
God the Abbot Sancho was the happiest of the men.
With the lights and with the candles to the court they ran in flight,
And him who in good hour was born they welcomed in delight.

"My Lord Cid," said the Abbot, "Now God has shed his grace!
Please accept my welcome, since I see you in this place."

And Cid who in good hour was born, "now answered here:
"My thanks to you, Don Sancho, your words content my ear.
For myself and for my servants provisions I must I make.
Since I depart in exile, these fifty coins please take.
If I may live my life-span, they will be doubled for you.
To the Abbey not a bit of trouble I will do.
For my lady, I give you a hundred coins again,
Herself, her ladies and daughters for you this year to maintain.
I leave two daughters with you, in years they have a few.
In your arms keep them kindly. I send them here to you.
Don Sancho please guard them, and of my wife take care.
If you want and lack anything never do despair.

Look to the provision I gave, I ask you to remember once more,
And for every coin you spend the Abbey will have four. "
And with a glad heart the Abbot made his consent clear.
And lady Jimena came with her daughters near.
Each had her lady-in-waiting, and once each had done,
Lady Jimena bent her knees for the Champion.
She kissed his hand, and cried as if she were torn!

"A blessing! A blessing! my Champion. In a good hour you were born.

And because of the evil minded, you are banished from the land.
"Oh Champion fair man I ask a favour from your hand!
See I kneel before you, and your daughters are here with me,
That have not seen many days, children they still be,
And these who are my ladies to serve my needs you know.
They will hear this also, before you are to go.
From you our lives will separate and remove,
But you gave us assistance, sweet Saint Mary's love you prove."

Cid, the nobly bearded, reached down to his daughter's arm,
And lifted her up again, and told her fear no harm.
And to his heart he pressed her, so great his love had grown,
And his tears fell fast and bitter, and painful was his moan:
"Jimena as my own spirit I love you, gentle wife;
But as well as you can see it, we must separate in our life.
I must go and you behind me on the land you must stay.
Please God and sweet Saint Mary we see each other again one day
As for marriage, my girls with my own hand I will give,
And thereafter in good fortune I hope you will live,
May they grant me, wife, much honoured, to serve you then once again."

Then a mighty feast they prepared for the Champion

The bells within San Pedro they rang with zeal.

That my Lord Cid is banished, men cried throughout Castile.
And some left their houses, from their lands some have run away.
A hundred and fifteen Knights were seen upon that day,
By the bridge across the Arlanzon together they went across.
One and all were calling on Cid of the Cross.
And Martin Antolinez has joined him with their power.
They sought him in San Pedro, who was born in a good hour.

When his company was growing, the great Cid of Vivar had heard,
Swiftly he rode to meet them, as his fame had spread the word.
When they come before him, he smiled at the band.
And one and all drew near him to kiss him on his hand.

My Lord Cid spoke so gladly: "Now to our God most high
I make my prayer that if I come to die,
I may repay your service, a house and land has its cost,
And return to you double any possessions you have lost."

My Lord Cid was merry, and his companions grew,
And they that come to him, all were merry too.
Six days of grace were over, and none were left but three,
Three and no more. Cid was warned, on his guard to be,
Because the King said, if after he found him on the land,
Then no gold or silver could redeem him from his hand.
And now the day was over and night began to fall
His knights he summoned, each and one and all:

"Hear me, my noble gentlemen, and distress will not be in your care.

Few goods are mine, yet I desire that each of you has his share.
As good men should, be prudent, when the birds crow in the day,
See that the horses are saddled, no hesitation or delay.

In San Pedro to say morning prayers the Abbot, on his knee,
Will say mass on our behalf to the Holy Trinity.
And when the mass is over, to our journey we attend,
Because the season of our suffering draws onward to an end.
And it is sure, moreover, that we have far to go."

Since Cid had ordered, they know they must do so.
Night passed, morning came, the birds were their alarms;
Immediately on the horses his companions threw their arms.
The bells rung for morning prayers with all the haste they may.
My Lord Cid and his lady to church they went their way.
On the steps Jimena threw herself, that stood before the shrine,
And to God passionately she said "God protect what's mine,
Our Father who are in Heaven, such glory is in You!
You made firmament and earth, and on the third day the sea too.
The stars and moon, You made, and the great sun to warm.
In the womb of Mary Mother, You took a human form.
You did appear in Bethlehem as it was Your will and choice.
And in Your praise and glory shepherds lifted up their voice.
And went from there to adore You, from Arabia and from

far,
Came three kings, Caspar, Melchior and Balthasar.
And gold and incense they offered eagerly.
You saved the prophet Jonah when he fell into the sea.
And you rescued Daniel from the lions in the cave.
And, moreover, in Rome city Saint Sebastian You did save.
From the sinful lying witness Saint Susanna you did ward.
And in years two and thirty, You walked the Earth, our Lord,
All men took notice, your miracles were divine.
From the stone, You made bread, and from the water you made the wine.
You raised up Saint Lazarus according to your will.
You let the Hebrews take You, to Calvary on the hill,
To a place called Golgotha, You, Lord, they crucified.

And the two thieves who were with You, they hanged on either side,
One is in heaven, the other down below,
A miracle you performed on the cross, we know where you go.
Longinus was blind, never had seen from his birth-year.
The side of our Lord Jesus he pierced with the spear.
The blood issued swiftly, on his garments it ran down the lace.
It stained his hands. He raised them and put them to his face.
Immediately his eyes were opened and in every way might see through.
He is ransomed from destruction for he straight believed in You.
From the grave You rose, and Hell you went to,
According to Your purpose, and its gates you overthrew,
To bring forth the Holy Fathers. The King of Kings, You are the chart,

And of all the world the Father, and You with all my heart
I worship and acknowledge, and for all you have won
That Saint Peter send my prayer quickly to Cid the Champion,
That God keep his head from evil; and the day comes to an end,
I hope He grants it to us that we meet in life again."

And now the prayer is over and the mass in its due course.
From church they left, and were about to get the horse.
Cid held Jimena, and his hand she kissed.
Bitterly she cried, in no way the deed she wished.
He turned to his daughters and he looked upon the two:
"To the Spiritual Father, have I presented you.
We must leave now. God knows when we shall meet again."

Weeping inconsolably - because never have you seen such pain
As the nail tears the flesh, from each other they did part.
And Cid with all his men prepared himself to start,
And as he waited for them again he turned his head,
Minaya AIvar Fanez then in good timing said:
"Cid! Where do you get your courage? Upon a happy day,
You were born. Let us take the road and quickly get away.
There is peace in this. Rejoicing out of these griefs will grow.
The God who gave us a spirit will give us aid also."

Don Sancho the good Abbot, Cid called him again to tell,
Watch and care for Jimena and her daughters as well,
And the ladies that were with them. That thry will have no lack
And a reward will be given. For this when he has come back,

Then Alvar Fanez spoke: "Abbot, if it coincides,
That men should desire to be in our company, and to ride,
Ask them follow but be ready for a long road to go
And that the heat and the desert; may overtake us so."

They all got on horseback, they let the reins go slack.
The time drew near when on Castile they had to turn their back.
Spinaz de Can, was the place that Cid had in sight.
Upon arrival, a great group of people welcomed him that night.
The next day at morning, he got on his horse once again,
And forward on from exile rode the Champion.
To the left, San Estevan the good town had appeal.
He marched through Alcobiella the border of Castile.
Over the highway to Quinea his course then had bent.
By Navas de Palos and over the Duero stream he went.
All night at Figueruela my Lord Cid did abide.
And very many people welcomed him on every side.

When it was night Cid lay down. In a deep sleep he fell,
And to him in a vision came the angel Gabriel:
"Ride, Cid, most noble Champion, because never did a knight
Ride forward at an hour, whose quality was so bright.
While you live good fortune will be with you and shine."
When he awoke, on his chest he made the holy sign.

He crossed himself, and offered God his soul again,
he was glad for the vision that had come into his brain.

The next day at morning they began again.
It should be known it came to an end, the term of their pain.

In the mountains of Miedes, Cid camped that night,
With the towers of Atienza, where the Moors reign in sight.

It was not yet sunset, and the day lingered still.
My Lord Cid gave orders to his men to fulfil.
Apart from the soldiers, and valiant men of war,
There were three hundred flags that each lance wore.

Feed all the horses early, so may our God give us speed.
Let whoever eat who needs it; and who will not, he gets on the steed.
We will pass the mountain ranges rough and of a dreadful height.
The land of King Alfonso we can leave behind tonight.
And whoever will seek us will find us ready then."

By the night the mountain ranges he had crossed-over with his men.
Morning came. From the hills downward they were about to go.
In a marvellous great forest Cid asked them halt below,
And to feed the horses early, he told them all aright,
In what way he was desirous that they should march at night.
They all were faithful men and gave agreement to;
The requests of their great captain it suited them all to do.
That evening every man was riding fit.
Cid decided to go at night so no man could get wind of it.
They marched all through the night and rested not at all.
Near Henares a town stood, Castejon it is called.

There Cid walked into a trap with his men, some say.

He hid there during the ambush until the breaking of the day.

Minaya Alvar Fanez advised him this and had planned:
"Cid, at the right time you circle round the band.
You with a hundred men will go and hold the rear.
Until we have we have drawn from Castejon all the bushmen here.
Give me two hundred men to then attack and to ride.
We will win much if your fortune and our God is on our side.

"You speak well, Minaya," the Champion said,
"You take the two hundred men, ride and have them led.
With Alvar Salvadorez, Alvar Alvarez shall advance,
And Galant Garcia, who is courageous with the lance.
Let them ride beside you Minaya, each valiant cavalier.
Let them ride forward and turn away from no one or from fear.
Out to Guadalajara, from Hita far and wide,
Forward to Alcala the city, let the warriors ride.
They return with all the winnings, let them be very sure,
Let them leave nothing behind them through terror of the Moor.
Here with a hundred lances in the rear I will remain,
And capture Castejon which has a good supply of food for us to gain.
If you come in any danger as you make the raid,
Send some swiftly here, and I will show all of Spain, how I gave aid."

Now all the men were chosen who on the raid should ride,
And those who in the rear with the Lord Cid should abide.
And now the dawn was breaking and the morning was

coming on,
And the sun rising. God! how beautifully it shone!
All men arose in Castejon, open they threw the gates;
And they went forward to oversee their farmlands and estates.
All were gone, and the gates stood open as they were thrown,
And all but a little was leftover of Castejon.
The people were scattered the whole town did not apprehend.
That out of the ambush came the Champion.
And without fail round Castejon he rushed along his way.
The Moors, both men and women, he took them for his prey,
And their flocks, he watched them as they strayed.
My Lord Cid Don Rodrigo straight for the gateway made,

And they that held it, when they saw the swift attack begin,
Ran in great fear, and through the gates Roy Diaz entered in,
With the naked sword in his hand, fifteen Moors he slew
Who he took away, In Castejon much gold, and silver too,
He captured. Then his knights brought the stuff.
To my Lord Cid they gave it. The win was not enough.

The two hundred men to pillage that rode out,
Sped fearlessly, and ravaged the country roundabout.
The banner of Minaya held high in esteem.
Then they took home the winnings up the Henares stream
Past Guadalajara. Winnings exceedingly great that they held,
Of sheep, cows and clothing and of other good wealth.
Straight away Minaya returned. No one dared a rear attack.
With the treasure they had taken his company turned their back.

From Castejon, where the Champion waited,
He rode out, and left the place guarded and gated.
With all his men around him he left the zone,
And with arms wide open welcomed Minaya home:

"You that come, Alvar Fanez, good lancer you are indeed.
Wherever I send you, I always wish you speed.
Put together all the winnings both mine and yours;
A fifth of it is yours, Minaya, distribute the rest of the wars."

"I thank you so much for it, illustrious Champion,
For what you give me, a fifth of all of what we've won,
The King Alfonso of Castile would be filled with astonishment.
I renounce it all in your favor, and give it with consent.
But I swear to God who lives in heaven, for our accomplishment,
That on my horse I go, and gallop in content,
Against the Moors, and until I wield my spear again,
And until from my elbow and the blade the blood does drain
Illustrious Cid, however small it is,

I will not take the value of a copper from what is his.
When through me, mighty treasure you have at your command.
I will leave the gift; until a time its needed, for now it's for your hand."

They put the prize together. My Lord,
Was deep in thought, He who in finest hour had ever held the sword,
News of his raiding found the King before long,
And Alfonso soon would seek him with his men to do him

wrong.
He asked his men to make the division fair,
And furthermore in writing give to each man his share.
The fortune of each Knight had done them very well,
One hundred coins of silver, to each of them fell,
And to each of the foot soldiers, half of that obtained.
A round fifth of the treasure for my Lord Cid remained.
But he could not sell it, or in gifts give it away.
No captives, men or women, he desired in his array.
And with the men of Castejon he said this with intent,
To Guadalajara some ambassadors he sent,
To find how much for the fifth part they would rate,
As they assessed it, his profit would be great.
Three thousand coins of silver the Moors agreed to pay.
Cid was pleased. And it was paid to him on the third day.
My Lord Cid determined with all his men of war,
That there within the castle, they would stay no more,
And that they would have held it, but with water it lacked,

"The Moors are friendly with the King; and even have made a pact,
We know he will pursue us, so we have to leave,
From Castejon; Minaya and my men, please listen to me,
Do not take it badly, what I say, because here we cannot stay.
The king will come to seek us, and he is not far away.
But to destroy the castle seems in no way good to me.
A hundred Moorish women in that place I will set free,
And from the hundred Moors, since there, as it befell,
I captured them, after all will speak of me well.
You all are paid; among you, no man yet to pay,
Let us tomorrow morning prepare to ride away.
Because against my Lord Alfonso the strife I do not want to stir."

What Cid said was pleasing to every follower.

They all departed rich men, from the hold that they had taken,
And the Moors both men and women blessed them over and over again.
Up the Henares they rushed and hard they rode so strong,
They passed through the Alcarrias, and swiftly marched along,
By the Caverns of Anquita they hurried on their way.
They crossed the stream into Taranz the great plain they,
Entered, And down through that region as hard as they might fare.
Fariza and Cetina Cid would seek shelter there.
And a great prize he captured in the country as he went,
Because the Moors had no inkling whatsoever of his intent.
On the next day marched onward the great Cid of Vivar,
And he went by Alhama, and down the vale far.
And he passed Bubierca, and Ateca likewise he passed,
And it was close to Alcocer that he would camp at last
Upon a rounded hill that was both strong and high.
They could not rob him of water; the Jalon river flowed right by.

My Lord Cid Don Rodrigo planned to storm Alcocer.
He pitched a strong encampment upon the hill there,
Some men were toward the mountains, some by the stream arrayed.
The gallant Cid, who in good hour had ever held the blade,
Asked his men near the water to dig a trench about their height,
So no man might surprise them by the day or night.

Some men might know that there Cid had taken stand,
And after the news of this went out through all that land,

How my Lord Cid the Champion got his footing secure,
He went forward from the Christians, into the land of the Moor,
In his presence no man dared to plough the farm,
Very merry with his men was the great Champion.

And Alcocer, Castle, a tribute he laid,
In Alcocer the citizens to Cid their tributes paid
And all the dwellers in Terrer and Teca furthermore.
And the townsmen of Calatayud, know well, it annoyed them sore.
Fifteen weeks he remained there, but the town didn't drop.
And when he saw it, Cid devised a plot.
Except one left pitched behind him, he put down every tent.
Then with his banner lifted, down the Jalon river he went,
With armour on and swords raised, a wise man would have a scare.
He went forward to ambush the men of Alcocer.
And when they saw the food, how glad was everyone!
Because by now my Lord Cid had none.
If he leaves one tent behind him, the burden cannot be light,
The others that he took with him ran like one in flight.
Let us now attack, great profit we shall gain.
We will win a mighty prize before we feel the pain.
By them who have their dwelling in the city of Terrer;
Because if by chance they take me, in the prize we cannot share.
That which had gone, double will be restored."

From the town of Alcocer in wild hasted they poured.

When Cid saw them unprepared, he acted as if he fled;
So with the enemy in confusion down the Jalon he sped.

"The enemy is escaping," They rushed forward great and small.
In the lust of conquest thinking of nothing else at all.
They left the gates unguarded, no one watched what they had done,
And then to them, rushed the great Champion,
He saw how they were tricked, and their hold now had a mighty space,
He made his men rush toward it. They spurred the horses with great pace.

"My Knights! Swiftly, every man strike in,
By the Creator's favour this battle we shall win."
And there they gave them a battle in the middle of the mead.
Ah God! We are rejoicing on this great morning indeed.
Cid and Alvar Fanez went straight on ahead;
You know they had good horses that to their liking sped.
'The townsmen and the castle, the way they broke,
Swiftly. And Cid's men merciless, came striking stroke on stroke,
In little time three hundred of the Moors blood they had spilled.
Loud was the shouting of the Moors in the ambush that were killed.
But they left them, they rushed on Right for the hold they made,
And at the gate they halted, each with a naked blade.
Then Cid's men came, as the enemy were all in flight.
You know Cid has taken Alcocer by such a sleight.

Where Cid's flag was visible Vermudoz went there,
On the highest part of the city he lifted it in air.
Out spoke Cid Roy Diaz, in a good hour he was born:

"To God in Heaven and all his saints, great thanks and praises sworn.
We will be better now our lodging for any Knight and steed."
Alvar Fanez and all my knights, now listen to me, give heed,
We have taken with the castle prizes manifold.
Dead are the Moors. Not many of the living I behold.

Surely we cannot sell them the women and the men;
And as for striking off their heads, we shall gain nothing then.
In the hold let us welcome them, because we have the upper hand.
When we lodge within their dwellings, they will do as we command."

Cid with all his other winnings lies in Alcocer.
He let the tent be sent for, that he left behind him there.
It annoyed the men of Teca, angry in Terrer they were;
You know on all Calatayud pain they did incur.
To the Sovereign of Valencia they sent the news with pace:
How the King Alfonso had been banished in disgrace
One who men call my Lord Cid, Roy Diaz of Vivar,
He came to lodge in Alcocer, and strong his lodgings are.
He drew them out to ambush; he has won the castle there.
If you do not send men you must lose both Teca and Terrer,
You will lose Calatayud as it cannot stand alone.
All things will go to ruin on the banks of the Jalon,

And round about Jiloca on the bank furthermore.
When the King Tamin had heard it, his heart was troubled sore:

"Here there are three Moorish kings. Let two leave without delay
With three thousand Moors and weapons for the fight ride right away;
Likewise they will be aided by the men of the frontier,
See that you take him living and bring him to me here.
He must pay for the realm's trespass until I am satisfied."

Three thousand Moors have mounted and set off to ride.
All of them go to Segorbe to lodge that night.
The next day they got ready to ride in the morning light.
In the evening to Celfa they came the night to spend.
And there they have determined for the borderers to send.
Little had they waited; from every side they came.
Then they went onward from Celfa (by the Canal of its name),
Never did they rest, but marched through the day's rain.
And that night to their lodging in Calatayud they came.
And they sent forward their messengers through the length of all the land,
A great and mighty army had gathered on their hand.
With the two Kings Fariz and Galve (these are the names they bear).
They will besiege my noble Lord Cid in Alcocer.

They pitched the tents and got into their lodgings there and then.
Strong grew their men's courage because there was a great store of them.
Moreover all the outposts, which the Moors set in array,
Marched to and fro in their armour night and day.
And with many outposts, and a powerful host of war.
From Cid's men, the water they cut off all the store.
My Lord Cid's brave men, great lust to fight they had,

But he who in good hour was born, told them Don't be mad.

For three full weeks together they hemmed the city in.
When three weeks were nearly over and the fourth would soon begin,
My Lord Cid and his men agreed upon this guise:

"They have cut us off from water; and our food must fail likewise.
They will not grant to us that we may run at night,
And very great is their power for us to face and fight.
My knights what is your will, say it now, what shall we do?
Then first to speak was Minaya the good knight and the true:

"Forward from Castile to this noble place we sped;
If with the Moors we do not fight, they will not give us bread.
Here are a good six hundred and some few more as well.
In the name of the Creator let us not dwell:

Let us strike tomorrow." The Champion then said:
"Minaya Alvar Fanez, my mind you must have read.
You have done yourself much honour, out of a great need you must.
Tell all the Moors men and women to go forward and to thrust,
Keep this secret so none will understand aright."

And then they armed them all through that day and through the night.
And the next day in the morning when soon the sun should rise,

Cid was armed and with him all the men of his enterprise.
My Lord Cid said to them, as you will hear:

"Let us all go forward, let no one stay in the rear,
Except two footsoldiers the gates to watch and shield.
They will capture this our castle, if we perish on the field;
But if we win, our fortunes will grow both great and fair.
Vermudoz, my banner I ask you now to bear,
As you are very courageous keep it without a stain.
But unless I order it, you will not loosen the rein."

He kissed Cid's hand. Forward he ran with the battle-flag to the gate,
They opened it, and outward in a great rush they made a break.
And all the outposts of the Moor observed them coming on,
They deserted them and back to their army they had gone.
What chaos among the Moors! To arm themselves they turned back.
With the thunder of the war-drum the earth was about to crack.

Now you see Moors arming, that swift their ranks did close.
Above the Moorish battle, two flags rose,
But out of the mingling banners the number who shall name?
Now all the squadrons of the Moors marching forward came.
Cid and all his men they might capture out of hand.

"My gallant men here in this place see that you firmly stand,
Let no man leave the war-ranks till my order I declare."

Vermudoz, found it too hard to bear,
He went forward with the banner high like the sun:
"May the Creator aid you, Cid the Champion,
Through the line of battle your banner I will take,
I will see how you bring support, you must for honour's sake."

The Champion said: "for charity, do not go to attack."
Vermudoz answered: "nothing shall hold me back."
Spurring the horse he hurled through the strong line of the foes.
The Moors welcomed him and struck him mighty blows,
And tried to take the banner from him, yet he delivered the mail.

The Champion said: "for charity I will help him prevail."

In front of their chests the war-shields were buckled strong,
The lances with the banners, they laid them in a row along,
And they had their faces over the bow,
Ready with brave hearts to strike them as they go.
Cid who in happy hour was born with a great voice gave a call:
"For the love of the Creator, strike them, and watch them all fall.
I am Roy Diaz of Vivar, Cid, the Champion."

At the rank where Vermudoz was the mighty strikes begun.

Three hundred lances raised and each bannered.
With one blow of every Moor his men hammered,
And when they turned to charge for the kill.
You would see many lances lowered and raised with great skill,
And many shields of leather pierced and shattered by the

strike,
And many coats of armour run through, pierced with the a spike,
And many a white banners covered red with blood,
Some running away, some scattered on the mud.

The Moors cried "Muhammed!" The Christians "Saint James of grace."
On the field thirteen hundred Moors were laid in a little space.

With his golden finish, how strongly Cid fought, the splendid knight.
And Minaya Alvar Fanez who with Zorita held the right,
And brave Martin Antolinez who stood there with pride,
And likewise Muno Gustoz, Cid's aide never tired!
Also Martin Gustoz who ruled Montemayor,
And with Alvar Salvadorez, Alvar Alvarez made the war
And Galind Garciaz the good knight that came from Aragon,
And Felez Munoz, Cid brother's son.
As many as were gathered there straight away come together as one,
And they sustained the standard and Cid the Champion.

Minaya Alvar Fanez the charger they had wounded with a blade,
The gallant group of Christians came to his aid.
His lance was split and straight away he placed his hand upon his sword,
How brave, as he dealt with the blows, and supported the Lord.
Cid, Roy Diaz of Vivar, saw how the matter stood.
He rushed to a governor that rode a charger good.
With his right hand he struck him, such a great strike with

the sword,
Cut through the waist; half of him was floored.
To Minaya Alvar Fanez he gave the steed.

"You are my right arm, Minaya, ride this horse with speed!
I will give you mighty support from this very day.
The Moors had not left the battle; they stood firm in their array,
And surely it's our duty to storm their line once more."

Minaya rode sword in hand; and on their host he waged great war,
Whoever he overtook, brought to death he did.
He who was born in happy hour, Roy Diaz, Lord Cid,
Three strikes against King Fariz. Twice the great strokes failed,
But the third found the vein. And down his shirt trailed.
A stream of red blood. To leave the field he wheeled his horse away.
By that one stroke the enemy was conquered in the fray.

Martin Antolinez led a heavy attack.
With his sword. On his helmet that even diamonds would crack.
The stroke went through the helmet because it reached to the flesh.
Let it be known, he did not dare delay for the man to strike afresh.
King Fariz and King Galve, beaten men they were.
What a great day for Christendom! Deterred the harrower.
The Moors fled. My Lord Cid's men still striking gave them chase.
Into Terrer went Fariz, and the people of the place,
None would welcome King Galve. As swiftly as they might
Onward to Calatayud he hastened in his flight.

And after him in full pursuit came the Champion.
Till they came to Calatayud that chase had not yet done.

Minaya Alvar Fanez had a horse that gallops well.
Out of the Moors four hundred and thirty that day fell.
And all his arms were bloody, because of his biting sword,
And streaming from his elbow downward the red blood poured.
Minaya said: "Now am I content; well will the news run,
To Castile, and make it known the battle my Lord Cid has won"

Few Moors are left, so many have already fallen dead,
And as many that we killed, as swiftly as they fled.
He who was born in happy hour gathered his men once again.
On his noble battle-charger rode the great Champion.
His hair was messy, in the name of God! But his great beard was fair.
His hood lay on his shoulders. In his hand his sword bare.
He looked upon his men and saw them drawing close:

"Since we have won such a battle, glory to God our almighty host!"
Cid and his men raided the encampment far and wide,
For the shields, the weapons and other wealth besides.
From the Moors horses they captured five hundred - ten.
And there was great rejoicing among those Christian men,
And of those Moors they took, fifteen were tolled.
They brought a countless treasure of silver and of gold.
Enriched were all those Christians with the goods that they had taken
And back to their castle they restored the Moors once again;
To give them something further, from what Cid

commandeered.
With all his men together the Champion was very cheered.

He gave some money, and the goods to be divided fair,
And a full hundred horses fell to Cid's fifth share.
In God's name! Every man he justly paid right,
Not only the footsoldiers but likewise every knight.
He who in happy hour was born formed well his government,
And all whom he brought with him were well content.

"Listen to me, Minaya, my right arm, you are mine.
From the wealth, with our army the Creator did assign,
Take in your hand whatever you deem good to choose.
To Castile I ask you go to carry there the news,
Of our triumph, to Alfonso the King who banished me,
A gift of thirty horses I desire to send in your company.
Every charger is saddled, each steed is bridled well.
There is a good war-sword hanging from every man who fell."

Minaya Alvar Fanez said: "I will do it with good cheer.
Of the gold and the fine silver, I observe the goods here.
Nothing is lacking. You will pay the money down
At Saint Mary's Church for masses fifty coins in Burgos town;
And to my wife and to my daughters, the remainder I leave there.
Let them offer day and night for me continually their prayer.
If I live, exceeding wealthy all of those ladies will be."

Minaya Alvar Fanez, left content it was such a sight to see.
They fed the horses, and the night fell.
"Go, Minaya, to the great land of Castile,

And to our well-wishers with a clear heart you can say:
'God granted us his favor, and we conquered on this day?'
If returning you find us here in this place, 'it is well;
If not, where you hear of us, go seek us where we dwell.
Because we must gain our daily bread with the lance and with the hand,
Since otherwise we perish here in a barren land.
And therefore as I think, we must therefore get away."
So was it, and Minaya went at the break of day.

But there behind the Champion did proudly stand.
And the country was unfruitful with exceedingly barren land.
Each day after my Lord Cid in that place spied,
On the Moors that dwelt on the border and outlanders outside.
King Fariz was healed. They held a meeting there,
Him, the men that dwelt in Teca and the townsmen of Terrer,
And the people of Calatayud, out of the three the fairest town.
As they have valued it and on parchment wrote it down.

Some of the goods in exchange for coins Cid set to sell.
And in regards to this, he sold them excellently well,
He paid his group! And made them wealthy then,
And you could not find a poor man, in his whole bunch of men.
In joy they were, those who serve a Lord of noble heart.
Finally my Lord Cid had chosen to depart,

The Moors, both men and women, cried in bitter woe:

"Lord Cid are you leaving? With our prayers you go.
With you we are full and well content."

Then my Lord the great Cid of Vivar, stood up and off he went,
The Moors, both men and women, their crying wasn't done.
He lifted up the banner, forward marched the Champion.
Down the Jalon he rushed, on he went rushing fast,
He saw birds which gave happy signals, from the stream that he passed.
The townsmen of Terrer were glad he had marched away,
And the dwellers in Calatayud were even more pleased than they.
But in the town of Alcocer there was grief to all and one,
Because many deeds of mercy to them Cid had done.
My Lord Cid rushed onward. Forward with speed he went,
It was near to the hill Monreal that he pitched up his tent.
Great is the hill, wondrous and very high likewise.
It should be known from there, they would fear no surprise.

And first he forced Doroca to pay him tribute,
And then charged on Molina and forced them to contribute,
Then Teruel who were against him, to submit he compelled,
And lastly, Celfa de Canal, within his power he held.

May my Lord Cid, Roy Diaz, always feel.
God's favour, Minaya Alvar Fanez has departed to Castile.
And to the King, thirty horses he took as a gift.
And when he saw, the King smiled and said "Who sent this?

Who gave you these, Minaya, to prosper, the Lord?"
"Cid Roy Diaz, who in good hour held the sword.
Since you banished him, by cunning has he taken Alcocer.
The King of Valencia lost them in a war to him there.
He asked that they surround him; from every water-well
They cut him off. He went forward from the citadel,

In the open field he fought them, and he beat them on that day,
Two Moorish kings he captured, sir, very mighty prey.
Great King, this gift he sends you. Your hands and feet also
He kisses. Show him mercy; as God would do so."

The King said: "It is over early for the banished one, without grace,
In his Lord's sight, to receive this by the end of three week's space.
But since 'it's Moorish goods I take it and consent.
That Cid has taken this, I am full and well content.
Beyond this Minaya your exemption I agree,
All my land, it's my honour to restore your liberty.
Go and come! My favour I grant to you once again.
But I have said nothing about Cid Champion.

"Beyond this, Alvar Fanez, I am urged to tell it,
That whoever is in my realm has to have a purpose to fit,
Let those, the brave and gallant, with Cid not wait.
I free them and exempt them both in body and estate."

Minaya Alvar Fanez kissed the King's hands, then:
Said: "Great thanks, to my rightful Lord I give you, King, again.
What you have done now, better than at a later hour.
We will labour to deserve it, if God will give us power."

The King said: "Minaya, for that, take peace with you on your way.
None will attack you, seek my Lord Cid without delay."

From him I urge you to tell, the one who in a good hour held the blade.
The hill, where his encampment in that season he has made,

While the Moorish men endure pain, while there are Christians still,
Forever they shall name in writing 'My Lord Cid's Hill.'
While he was there great damage to the moors he made,
And an accolade to the whole valley of Martin he laid.
And to Zaragoza the news of him went,
Which didn't please the Moors; actually rather they had anger to vent.
For fifteen weeks together my Lord Cid stayed to wait.
When the good knight saw how greatly Minaya was late,
Forward with all his men on a night march he tried.
And he left all behind him, and deserted the mountain side,
Beyond the town of Teruel good Don Rodrigo went.
In the pine grove of Tevar Roy Diaz pitched his tent.
And all the lands around him he attacked in the raid,
And on Zaragoza city a heavy honour laid.

When this he had accomplished and three weeks had made an end,
Out of Castile Minaya went to Cid his good friend.
Two hundred knights were with him that had fastened their weapons.
You know well that there were many foot-soldiers in his possession.
When Cid saw Minaya coming closer to his view,
With his horse at a full gallop to embrace the man he flew.
He kissed his cheek, and his eyes in that hour kissed Cid.
And then all things he told him, because nothing from him he hid.
Then he smiled, beautifully upon him, the good Champion:
"God and his righteousness, the divine greatly praised for what He's done.

While you live, Minaya, you go well, I claim."

My God! How happy was the army that Minaya came,
Because when he had left them, he spread the news happily,
From man to man, family to family.

But God! What a glad face Cid the fair-bearded wore,
That fittingly Minaya and the masses paid for,
And of his wife and daughters all of the state displayed!
God! How content was he by that! What a great cheer he made!
"Ha! Alvar Fanez, many days may your life be.
What fair despatch you have made! you are worth more than we."

And he who in good hour was born delayed in no way then,
But he took two hundred knights, and all well chosen men;
And onward when the evening fell, to raid they made haste.
At Alcaniz the meadows the Champion laid the waste,
And went to all places around to ravage and ransack.
On the third day to where he came from, again Cid turned back.

Throughout the whole country the news of them flew.
It grieved the men of Huesca and the people of Monzon too.
They were glad in Zaragoza since the tribute they had paid,
Because of the victory at Roy Diaz's hand not a bit they were afraid.

Then back to their encampment they rushed with all they could grab.
The men were very merry because of everything they now had.

Cid was exceeding glad; Alvar Fanez liked it well.
But the great Cid smiled, because there at ease he could not bear to dwell.

"Ha! All my knights, to you the truth I will confess:
Who stays in one place and delays, his fortune will grow less.
Tomorrow morning let us prepare to ride with pace,
Let us march and leave forever our encampment in this place."

Through the closest river the Lord Cid had gone.
Then to Huesca and to Montalban he hastily marched on.
And then ten full days after that raid they were to ride.
The news to all quarters went flying far and wide,
How that the Exile from Castile great harm to them had been done.
Afar into all quarters did the news of him run.
They brought the message to the Count of Barcelona's hand,
How Cid Roy Diaz was over running all the land.
He was angered, an insult he took it as.
The Count was a great boaster but an empty word he has:

"Great wrongs he has put upon me, he of Vivar, Cid.
Much shame within my very palace to me he did,
He gave no satisfaction when he struck my brother's son,
And the lands of my holding now he does over-run.
I did not challenge him, our pact of peace I did not overthrow,
But since he seeks it of me, to demand it I will go."

He gathered his powers that were exceeding strong,
Great troops of Moors and Christians in lines so long.
After the Lord Cid of Vivar, they went on their way,

Together on the march they, went for two nights and a day.
Finally in Tevar's pine grove they had overtaken Cid,
So eager were they to take him captive and remove him from the grid.

My Lord Cid Don Rodrigo with great goods he went.
From the ridge to the valley until he finished the descent.
And in that place they found him and gave Count Don Remond's word.
My Lord Cid sent a reply, after the message he had heard:

"Say to the Count that it is best his anger should now cease.
No goods of his I carry. Let him leave me in peace."

To this the Count gave his answer: "Not until the matter ends.
For what was and is of evil he shall give me full amends.
The Exile will display swiftly whom he has sought to sleight.'
Back rushed the ambassador as quickly as he might.
And then my Lord Cid of Vivar knew how the matter stood,
And that without a battle there was no option to run if they could.

"Put aside your goods now every one of you Knights,
And raise your weapons, and prepare for one of the worst fights.
Against us, Count Don Remond will deliver a strong battle;
Great troops of Moors and Christians he brings with him like cattle.
He will not for any reason without fighting let us go.
So here we will give them a battle since they pursue us so.
So get your armour on and strap the horses tight.
Down the hill they come in trousers and their saddles light,
And their straps are loose. Each man of us has a Galician

shell,
And moreover with the long boots our trousers covered well.
We should beat them, although we are outnumbered by his peers.
Before they reach the boarder, let us attack them with spears.
Each of you strike three saddles, the horses will come and go.
Who the man was he hunted, Remond will know
This day in Tevar's pine grove, who could take from me my goods."

When Cid had said this, all put on the battle hoods.
They had their weapons held, and each had taken a horse.
They observed the French looking army, down the hill make its course.
And at the end of the descent, close to the level land,
Cid who in good hour was born, gave the command.
To charge at them, and this his good men performed with all their heart,
With the banners and the lances they nobly played their part.
Striking some, and others overthrowing them with their might.
He who was born in happy hour had conquered in the fight.
There he took Count Don Remond as a prisoner of the war,
And his war-sword worth a thousand coins or more.

By the victory, much honour to his beard he did.
And then the Count to his own tent was taken by Cid.
He told his aides to guard him. And then he left them.
From every side together around him came his men.
Cid was glad, so great was the reward of that defeat.
Because for Lord Cid Don Rodrigo they prepared a great

stock of meat.
But for the Count Don Remond, he gave no store.
To him they brought some scraps, and placed them on the floor.
He would not eat, and all of them he mocked with distain:

"I will not eat a mouthful for all the wealth of Spain;
Rather will I lose my body for the sake of my soul,
Since I was beaten in the battle by such a scruffy troll."

My Lord Cid Roy Diaz, this is what he said:
"Drink the wine, Count, and please also eat your bread.
If you do this, you will no longer be a captive then;
If not, you will never see Christendom again."

"You eat, Don Rodrigo, and prepare to sleep sweet.
Myself I will let perish, and nothing I will eat."
And in no way could they make their convict,
Eat a mouthful while they allocated all from the conflict.

"Count, eat something," Lord Cid spoke,
"If you do not eat, you will never look again at Christian folk.
If you eat until my will is satisfied,
You, Count, and, moreover, two noblemen beside,
I will grant your liberty and set you free."
And when the Count heard it he was as glad as could be.

"Cid, if you will keep this promise that you give,
Forever after, I will marvel as long as I shall live."

"Eat then, Count; when you have eaten your dinner right through,
I will set at liberty you and the other two.

But all in the open battle you did lose and I did earn,
Know that not one penny's worth to you I will return,
Because I need it for these men and you can see their aren't a few,
They will be paid with what I win from others the same as from you.
With the Holy Father's favour we will live after this, as wise,
Banished men who have not got any grace in the King's eyes."

The Count was so glad. He asked for water to clean his palms.
And they brought it to him, quickly and calm.
The Count of Barcelona began to eat his fill
With the men Cid had given him, and God! With what a will!

He who in happy hour was born, to the Count ate near:
"Ha! Count, if now you do not dine with exceedingly good cheer,
And to my satisfaction, here we will delay,
And in no manner will we go onward straight away."

The Count then said: "Right gladly and according to my mind!"
With his two knights at that season in a mighty rush he dined.
My Lord Cid was well content, and all his eating he viewed,
Because the Count Don Remond his hands he nimbly used.

"If you are pleased, my Lord Cid, we are ready to leave,
Ask them to bring us our horses; we will mount them speedily.

Since I was the first Count, to ever have dined with a will so glad,
It shall not be forgotten what joy within I had."

They gave him three horses. Each had a noble saddle.
Good robes of fur they gave them, and jackets fair as well.
Count Don Remond rode onward with a knight on either side.
To the camp's end the Castilian went along with them for the ride.

"Ha! Count, you may depart to freedom fair and frank;
For what you have left with me I now have you to thank.
If the desire to avenge is present in your mind,
Send to me beforehand when you come for me to find.
Either you will leave your goods or part of mine you'll seize."

"Ha! my Lord Cid, you are secure, be wholly at your ease.
Enough I paid you, until all this year is gone.
As for coming out to find you, I will not think thereon."

The Count of Barcelona went onward. God the speed that he made.
Turning his head, he looked at them, because he was much afraid.
In case my Lord Cid regretted it; which the gracious Cid,
Would not have done for all the world. Bad deeds he never did.
The Count is gone. He of Vivar turned back again,
He began to be very merry, as he mingled with his men.
Very great and wondrous were the goods that they had won in this war,
So rich were his companions that they couldn't carry more.

POEM 2

THE MARRIAGE OF CID'S DAUGHTERS

Here my Lord Cid of Vivar begins a new song.
Through the town of Alueat, my Lord Cid was made strong,
He left Zaragoza and the lands that nearby lie,
And all the coasts of Montalban and Huesca he passed by,
And to the salty ocean he began the way by force.
In the East the sun arises; to there he turned his course.
On Jerica and Almenar and Onda he laid his hand,
Round about Borriana he conquered all the land.

God helped him, the Creator in Heaven that dwell
Beside these Murviedro Cid had taken as well.
To know the Lord was on his side, Cid held it clear.
In the city of Valencia he arose with little fear.

It angered them in Valencia. It gave them no delight,
They planned to surround him. They then marched at night,
They pulled up at Murviedro, to camp as morning broke.
My Lord Cid observed it and therefore he spoke:

"Father in Heaven, mighty thanks I give you now.
In their lands we dwell and they think we play them foul;
We have drunk their liquor, from their bread we make our food so.
If they come to surround us, justly they do so.
Without a fight this matter in no way will be paid.
Let messengers go to seek them and this will give us aid;
Let them go to them in Jerica and all that are,
In Alueat, and Onda, likewise let them go to Almenar.

Let the men of Borianna, now at once come in.
In this place a battle, we shall certainly begin.
I trust much will be added to our gain in this way."

They will attack together our host on the third day.
And he who in good hour was born began to make his meaning clear:

"So may the Creator aid us, my men listen and hear.
Since we have left fair Christendom - we did not as we would,
We had no other option - God be praised that our fortune has been good.
The Valencians surround us. If here we would remain,
They must learn from us a lesson, exceedingly in its pain.

"Let the night pass and morning come, make sure you are prepared.
With arms and horses, we will go forward toward the leader of theirs'.
Like men out in exile, into a strange empire,
There it will be determined who is worthy of his hire."

Minaya Alvar Fanez, listened to all he said:
"Champion, with you I will go wherever led.
Give me a hundred knights, you keep the others, attack from the front,
While my hundred storm from the rear with a shunt."

What he had said filled Cid with good cheer
The morning came and they put on their battle gear.
Each man knew and understood his task.
At the break of day, they and the Lord Cid went forward fast.

"In God's name and Saint James', my knights, strike hard, this is war,
The Lord Cid am I, Roy Diaz of Vivar!"

You will see tent-ropes broken throughout,
Tent-posts bent, and pegs: without.
So many Moors, trying to recover strength,
But Alvar Fanez continued the attack at length.
So bitterly it grieved them, they had to flee and yield.
They put their trust in their horses, and finally fled the field.
Two Morisco Kings they had put to death;
And all the way to Valencia the chased until out of breath.
My God, all the goods Lord Cid had taken.
They ravaged the country and then turned back again.
They brought to Murviedro the goods of the foes.
And there great rejoicing in the city arose.
They took over Cebolla and all the lands near.
In Valencia they knew not to resist, due to fear.

The news of Lord Cid became known, and on all sides spread,
His renown grew, and beyond the sea it sped.
His companions were glad, and so was he,
That God had given him assistance and granted victory.
They sent forward their warriors, and night they persevered,
Until they reached Cullera, and in Jativa they appeared.
And downward even to the town of Denia they went
And the Moorish land by the sea he took, it was magnificent.

Penacadell, outbound and the entrance they had taken,
When Cid took Penacadell, it was great grief and pain.
To those who dwell, in Cullera and in Jativa,
Sorrow fell, without measure and in Valencia as well.
Cid conquered, and for three years those Moorish towns

was his abode,
Winning much; in the day he rested, and at night was on the road.

Those from Valencia must have felt very sore,
But they didn't dare go against him and make war.
He destroyed all their gardens, total destruction made;
The years that followed their harvest was decayed.
The Valencians cried out, they were in such a sorrow mood,
None could find in any quarter, any sort of food;
No father could aid the son, and no son could aid the dad,
No man could comfort man, such hardship they had.
A lack of bread, seeing their wives and children grow weak,
They saw their own affliction and no hope they could seek.

To the King of Morocco the news had gone.
But against the Lord of Monte Claros a great war he was on.
He gave no advice, and did not offer them any aid.
Of course Lord Cid had heard this, and such happiness he displayed;
From Murviedro he marched onwards by night.
He was in the fields of Monreal at the breaking of the light.
Through Aragon the news was published, and Navarre,
And throughout the land of Castile the news spread so far:
Whoever wanted to put poverty aside and gain riches,
Sought Cid, for the soldier's life in ditches.

It was his desire to see Valencia go down,
So to all the Christians he may free the town

"Valencia to conquer, who would like to march with me,
Do not come unless your choice is free.
Nothing, no comfy house should compel him to stay,

To Canal de Celfa in three days we will leave with no delay."

So Lord Cid had spoken, the loyal Champion,
He turned back to Murviedo that he had taken.

It became known in all quarters of the world, so many wanted in,
There was no delay in this, masses of Crowds flocked to him.
Good Christians, the news went far and wide;
And more men came to him than departed from his side.
Cid of Vivar, what a great growth in riches he had.
When he saw the men assembled, he began to be very glad.
My Lord Cid, Don Rodrigo, would not delay.
He marched against Valencia and struck it straight away.
Cid surrounded it; until he closed in, and circled about.
He stopped all their incomings, and he checked their goings out.
To seek for aid, he gave them a little grace;
And nine full months later he sat down before the place,
And when the tenth month was coming, they yielded easily.
What a great triumph and joy there was in the city.

When Lord Cid took Valencia and within the town he had won.
All of his men became knights with horses, before on foot they had gone.
The worth of all the gold and silver who could declare?
They all were rich together as many as there were.
For himself Cid Rodrigo took a fifth of all they could count,
And thirty thousand coins was the total amount.
Who could imagine the other treasure and great joy as well,
Of his men, when the royal-flag was hung over the citadel.

Cid and his companions rested on that day,
To the King of Seville the news found its way.
Valencia has been taken; he holds it no more.
With thirty thousand armed men he came to bring them war.
Close to the battle field they came strong and proud.
But Cid the long-beard overthrew that crowd.

To Jativa in a haste they rushed without stopping,
You would have seen all bedlam in Jucar by the crossing,
There the Moors drank water but sorely against their will.
With only three bruises on him escaped the ruler of Seville.
And then with all the winnings Cid came home again,
So great his wealth had grown, since Valencia's town was taken.
But the goods of that battle were greater yet, you should know,
That a hundred silver coins to each man would go.

How great was that noble man's fortune now you may lightly guess.
And among those Christians there was exceeding happiness
As Lord Roy Diaz was born in a season of good grace.
Now his beard was growing; taking more space on his face.
Cid spoke, and from his mouth began to orate,

"I love King Alfonso, the King who banished me from beyond the gate,"

And resting in Valencia, the Lord Cid did abide,
With Minaya Alvar Fanez who would never leave his side.
Those who were banished, left a mighty hoard,
Of goods. To all men in Valencia, Cid the Lord,
Gave houses and possessions and they were very glad.

All men of Cid's were happy with what they had.
And those who had just come, were content, everyone,
My Lord Cid saw it plainly that they would happily get things done.
With the goods that they had taken, if unhindered they should go.
Lord Cid gave his order, and Minaya told them so,
If anyone with him there, has more than any other man,
And tried to make his leave in secret and fail to kiss his hand,
If they overtake him and caught him as he fled,
They would seize his goods and surely cut off his head.

And so! All was well looked after, advice he took again,
With Minaya Alvar Fanez, and so he said: "My friend,
I would like to know, Minaya, what the number may be
Of my men, as at present, that have gained and ran from me.
I will put it down in writing, first I will take a scan,
If one has left in secret, I would not miss the man.
To me and my companions, his goods will be restored,
All they who guard Valencia and keep the outer ward.

"The advice should be well welcomed," said Minaya to them all.
He told them to meet together at the palace, in the hall.
When he found them all together he took a count,
Vivar's great Cid had with him three thousand and thirty on account.
His heart was glad, he had a smile on his face.

"Thanks to God, Minaya, and to Mary Mother's grace.
In Vivar, we had a less power.
Wealth we have now, and will have greater at some hour.
Minaya, if it pleases and seems good to you,

To Castile I want to send you, with our possessions. Please do,
Go to King Alfonso, who is my Lord by right,
Out of the great goods we have won here in the fight.
I would give him 100 horses, which to him you can now take,
Kiss his hand and sincerely plead with him for the sake,
Of my wife Ximena and the two, maids made from the blood of me,
If it is now his pleasure that they be brought to me.
I will send for them, this is how my message runs:
The lady of Lord Cid and her maids, the little ones,
Should be sought for by men, who believe they have the right,
And shall come to the strange country we have conquered with our might."

Minaya answered: "Yes, and they have to have a good heart."
After they had said this, they got ready to depart.
For Alvar Fanez Cid declared one hundred men agreed,
To do his will, and serve him on the journey at his need.
And he gave San Pedro fifty thousand silver coins sure,
And to the Abbot Sancho a full five hundred more.

While they were joyous, news came from the East,
About the Bishop Don Jerome, all men called the priest.
Who had exceeding knowledge, and prudent views,
A mighty man of valor on foot or horse, however you choose.
The news of Cid's deeds, he sought to confirm and procure,
And he yearned completely, for a battle with the Moor.
If, to fight and wound with his hands he could get,
As a Christian he would never need a reason for regret.
When my Lord Cid heard it, he was delighted,

Minaya Alvar Fanez, by his side was excited,
The Lord God has given us aid, let us give Him thanks again.
From Valencia a bishop comes to join my men,
I will pass this news on to them, with a Christian zeal.
That news which you have brought to Castile.

Alvar Fanez was glad when Cid spoke.
Don Jerome joining was a happy moment, and is no joke.
In Valencia great riches they have given to his hand.
God! how merry was all Christendom now within the land
From Valencia a bishop of reverence and grace they had!
Minaya went on his way, while being exceedingly glad.

Valencia left as a peaceful estate.
Minaya Alvar Fanez went to Castile and departed straight;
His halts I will pass over, nor renew them to the mind.
He sought Alfonso the King, but where was he to find?
The King had gone to Sahagun before a little space,
But on his way back to Carrion; he might find him in that place.
Minaya Alvar Fanez was glad when this was known.
And with this news he departed to Carrion.

Now with the mass was over, see Alfonso arise,
And Minaya Alvar Fanez came there in a noble disguise.
In the presence of the people on his knee he knelt,
He fell at Don Alfonso's feet, and bitter tears he dealt.
He kissed his hands; giving the King lovely words and said why he came:
"A favour my Lord Alfonso for the Creator's aim!

My Lord Cid of the battles, has kissed my hands,
Your hands and your feet likewise, as a noble Lord demands.

If you favour him, God's favour comes to you from above.
He was sent in to exile and no one showed him love,
Though in strange lands he thrived, in Jerica he won in war,
And Onda, so they call it; and also Almenar,
And likewise Murviedro – as a great town it is known,
And he has taken Cebolla and further Castejon
And he has stormed Penacadell, such a place of power.
He is the master of Valencia and all these places at this hour.
With his own hand the great Champion a bishop has ordained.
He has thought battles and in each a victory he has gained.
The gift of the Creator was once a very mighty prey,
Can you observe the tokens of the truth that I say?

Here are a hundred horses that in strength and speed excel;
With reigns and with saddle each one is furnished well.
"I kiss your his hands and offer these of my own accord.
To be your servant, and serve you as my Lord."

The King lifted his right hand and crossed himself thereon:
What a wonderful blessing the Champion has done.
I am well pleased in spirit, Saint Isidore give you speed!
I am glad the Champion comes and does me such a deed.
I accept the gift of horses that you have sent"
The King was gladdened, and Ordonez was content;

"It seems to me to be, that in those lands the Moors are gone,
Since God's will works through Cid the Champion."

To the Count the King gave a reply: "What one man can do!
Certainly he has done me a greater service even than you."

And then Minaya said: "Cid desires a favour from you,
For his wife lady Ximena and daughters, the two,
That they may leave the convent where he left them before he begun,
And rush to Valencia to the noble Champion."

The King said in answer: "His wish is my command,
And they will be escorted, and protected as they travel through my land.
From insult and dishonour and whatever harm may be.
And when these ladies have reached my kingdom's boundary,
Take care how you serve them, them and the Champion.
Now listen to me, my servants, to what else shall be done:
I seek that Roy Diaz suffers no loss at all,
And therefore to his men, and to Cid their Lord, as they call,
I restore that which I seized, their possessions and their fee,
Let them keep their land, wherever Cid may be,
Freedom from harm, the safety of these people I reward,
This I do so they may render service to their Lord."

Minaya Alvar Fanez kissed the King's hand straight away.
And the King smiled at him and what else did he say?

"Whoever desires to serve the Champion, and wants to ride,
As for me, he has permission, and God's grace is on his side.
The fame of Cid the Champion grows great on every side,
And we might wed his daughters, if our needs are satisfied.
We dare not undertake this project ourselves alone;
Cid is from Vivar, and we are Counts of Carrion."

They hatched that plot between them, and to none they said
a thing.
Minaya Alvar Fanez finally left the King.

"How is it going, Minaya? Does the Creator give you
grace?
Take it as a sign, as I deem it, he may help you in this case.
If you take the ladies, serve them in all they desire.
From there to here, grant them all that they require.
The Champion will take them under his wing from then
on."
And after hearing this, from the court Minaya was gone.

And so the Heirs of Carrion did what they were told with
consent.
Along with Minaya Alvar Fanez in his company they went:

"In all things you exceed; likewise in this excel,
As much as you can my Lord Cid of Vivar, for us as well.

With Minaya rushing to San Pedro where the three ladies
are.
There was great rejoicing when they saw him from afar.

"I greet you, lady Ximena. God helped you prosper where
you dwell,
And likewise your daughters, the noble children as well.
In the city where he resided the Lord Cid has fair,
Good health and riches that are beyond compare.
Your freedom the King gave as a gift to me,
To take you to Valencia our land with no fee.
If Cid could see you well and unharmed again,
He would rejoice, and would have no pain."

"As the Creator decides," Lady Ximena said,

Minaya Alvar Fanez sent three horsemen to go ahead,
To Cid in Valencia and give the word.

"Tell the Champion, who the Lord God has preserved,
That his wife and daughters the King has released in to my hands,
And has ordered an escort for us, as we travel through his lands.
Fifteen days from today, if God keep us in his care,
With his wife and with his daughters I will come to him there,
With the noble ladies and any servants that may be."

The riders have gone ahead, and to the matter they will see.

Minaya Alvar Fanez was in San Pedro and as he took the road,
You could see all the households swarming him as he rode;
To my Lord Cid of Vivar in Valencia, as they went,
They told Alvar Fanez that they offered Cid encouragement.
To them Minaya replied. "That I will gladly do."
And five hundred sixty horsemen swelled his retinue.
He had brought a hundred with him under his command,
To accompany the ladies, they arrayed a noble band.
Minaya gave five hundred to the Abbot for war.
I will tell how he expended the other five hundred and sixty more.

Ximena the good lady and likewise her daughters,
And those that served her, the women of her orders,
To deck out all those ladies, Minaya did prepare,
With the best apparel in Burgos, that he could discover there,
The horses likewise that were fair to see,

When he had decked the ladies in this manner beautifully.
Good Minaya got ready, to ride along the street,
The suddenly Raquel and Vidas, fell on the floor at his feet:

"A favour! True knight, Minaya! Cid took our aid,
He has ruined us, unless the amount to us is paid,
We can't write off the repayment!" - "I will talk to Cid,
If God takes me there, and say to return the favour, for everything you did.
Raquel and Vidas replied: "The Creator should grant it so,
If not, we will leave Burgos town, and in search of him we'll go."

Minaya Alvar Fanez continued to San Pedro and had barely gone,
When many people came around him as he started to ride on.
When parting from the Abbot, you could see great grief there:

"Minaya Alvar Fanez, God keep you in his care.
The hands of the good Champion, I ask you kiss for me,
I hope he keeps the promise we made in history,
And always endeavours to get it done,
This will increase the honour of Cid the Champion."

"I will do it gladly," Minaya straight away replied,
He then left the Abbot and continued on his ride,
And with him went the ladies, on their needs he was to wait,
Through the King's realm, the escort he gave was very great.
From San Pedro to Medina, in five days' time that had

passed,
The ladies and Alvar Fanez arrived in Medina at last!

I will tell you about the horsemen that brought the news through.
When my Lord, good Cid of Vivar, learnt of what they knew,
His heart was glad and merry, his voice he lifted straight:

"Who sends this noble message, his presence I await,
Munio Gustoz, Pero Vermudoz, I think of you,
And Martin Antolinez from Burgos, the tried and true,
And Jerome the bishop also, not many like he,
With a hundred riding, ready to fight if the need may be.
Through Saint Mary's to Molina further onward you will descend;
Avelgalvon holds there more of my men and my friend,
With another hundred horsemen he will watch you on your way,
Go forward to Medina with all the speed that you may,
With Minaya Alvar Fanez my wife and daughters there,
If you happen to discover them as the messengers declare.
Bring them here to me, In Valencia I will stay,
The saddled the horses for riding, to journey on their way,
With utmost speed they hastened, their march they would not delay,
They passed by Saint Mary's, at Fronchales they rested for the day.
Into Molina, onward they went,
The Morisco Avengalvon got news, and with joy he made his descent:
"Are you the servants of my heart's dearest friend?
I welcome it gladly, my joy is great and I am content."

And Muno Gustoz answered, "My Lord Cid sends you his command,
That with a hundred horsemen you will serve from your hand.
In the city of Medina, with his wife and daughters near,
You will go to them straight away and return with them here,
Even to Valencia from them you will not depart."

Avengalvon gave his answer: "I will do it with all my heart."
That night he chose to escort, a mighty group they were,
In the morning he was leading them, almost like a chauffeur.
They asked for a hundred; two hundred had he too,
They crossed the mountains, steep and high, passing through.
And over the woods of Toranz, so strong they had no dread.
And along through Arbujuelo down the vale they sped.
Now round about Medilla they watched on every side,
Minaya Alvar Fanez eyes were open wide,
Observing the armed train,
He was afraid and sent two knights to make the meaning plain.
They did not delay, to discover his desire their hearts were happy.
One stayed, to Alvar Fanez the other came snappy:

"Men sent by Lord Cid, Pero Vermudoz, the height of rank in that crew,
And likewise Muno Gustoz that frankly loves you too,
And Martin Antolinez that was born in Burgos town,
And Don Jerome the Bishop of honourable renown.
Avellgalvon the Castellan brings his host with these,
In eagerness the honour of my Lord Cid will increase.

They march along together, soon they will come."
Minaya said: "Onward let us ride." And swiftly this was done,
No delay, a hundred most splendidly dressed,
Going forth on noble horses with embellishments of the best.
Bells hung upon them, the knights wore,
Bright belt buckles, and carried lances which flew the flags of war,
Alvar Fanez' wisdom to all they might reveal,
And in disguise with those ladies he had released from Castile.
All those observing, to the army ran,
And lifted up their weapons, a mighty cheer began.
Merriment, there was, when all those who raise,
Good cheer, came to Minaya, and all gave him praise.
And when Avengalvon came, Minaya saw, and with good style,
Forward he went to embrace him, with such a big smile.
On the shoulder he saluted him, as this was still his way:

"Minaya Alvar Fanez! What a glorious day!
You bring these ladies here, we have done such a great thing,
The fighting Cid, his wife, and the daughters of his kin.
We have to give you honour as his fortune has grown great.
Even if I wished him ill, we cannot diminish his estate;
He will have always our aid, either in peace or in war,
Any man who does not know this truth, is a fool therefore."

On Minaya Alvar Fanez's lips a smile broke out:
"Haha Avengalvon. You are his friend no doubt.
If God takes me to Cid alive and I see him too,
The things you have done for us will greatly profit you.
Let us go take our rest, supper they have made ready there."

Avengalvon gave his answer: "This is a courtesy most fair;
I will repay it double, on the third morning fall."

To the town they went, Minaya provided for them all.

The escort that came with them, they were gladdened when they saw.
Minaya the King's messenger commanded to withdraw.
The Lord Cid in Valencia was greatly honoured then,
When they gave such entertainment in Medina to his men.
The King paid for all. Minaya therefor did not have to pay.
Finally the night was over, and then came the break of day.

They attended mass, and after away they rode at last,
They rushed from Medina, over the Jalon they passed,
Down the Arbujuelo, with such pace they ride,
In haste through the meadows of Toranz they crossed from side to side,
They came to Molina where Avengalvan was the Lord,
Bishop Jerome, a Christian worthy of his deed and his word,
Escorted the three ladies whether day or by night,
And he led a good charger with his armour on his right.
And he and Alvar Fanez rode together as thus,
They entered Molina the rich and glorious,
And loyally Avengalvon the Moor served them there,
To the height of their desire, nothing they couldn't share:

He even asked men to remove the horseshoe from the steed.
Minaya and the ladies, God! He honoured them indeed
They placed them on horseback when the next morning fell.
All the way to Valencia, loyally he served them well.

The Moor spent from his own, because he took nothing from the men,
To such honourable revelry and festivities he treated them.
They came close to Valencia, three miles away now they stand,
To my Lord Cid who in good hour had circled around the land,
In the city of Valencia the news of this was his,
Nothing had ever gladdened him as much as this,
Because now came the good news of those who he loved,
Straightaway the told two hundred horsemen to go forward from above,
To the good ladies and Minaya a fair reception was offered,
But he remained in Valencia to watch it and meet them afterward,

Because he knew that Alvar Fanez would return with due care,
And now the two hundred welcomed Minaya back there.
To the ladies and the daughters and all within the band,
Cid had a plan, to take them in the group, and this was his command,
As they went toward the citadel, and the towers that were so high,
And the gates that none could enter and none could depart by.
He asked to camp there, where a little time before,
From the King of Seville a place he had taken, when he beat him in a war.

At the gateway of Valencia, where none dared to cause him woe,

To his wife and daughters, his winnings, he desired to finally show.

When the ladies with great honour the host had welcomed home,
First into the city came the Bishop Don Jerome.
He left his horse; to chapel straightaway the Bishop went,
With all men that he could gather who had the same intent,
All clad with crosses of silver, once again,
They greeted good Minaya and the ladies accompanied by the men.
Cid who was born in a happy hour delayed little there,
He put on his coat, his beard was long and fair,
On Bavieca his horse, a saddle and coverings they threw,
Cid took wooden weapons; and forward on the horse he flew.
Bavieca jumped, and my God he could run,
It was rare to see, marvelled everyone.
From that day Bavieca, in all of Spain had renown,
When the run was over, from the horse Cid got down,
And rushed to his lady and daughters, to greet.
When lady Ximena saw him she threw herself at his feet:

"All in good season, and to your favour, Champion!
You have taken me away from insults that were done.
Look at me, Lord! And look at my daughters, as at me.
By God's help and yours, they are noble, and gentle as can be."

And Cid straightaway embraced them, mother and daughters,
Such joy they had, that from their eyes began waters,
His men rejoiced, the posts, they pierced them with the spear,

He who held the sword in a good time, listen to what he said and hear.

"Oh you my Lady Ximena, beloved and honoured wife,
And you two, my daughters that are my heart and life,
The city of Valencia you will now enter in,
The fair estate you will see, for you, was mine to win."

They kissed his hands straight away, the Lady and daughters did the same,
So with exceeding honour to Valencia they came.

With them the Lord Cid hurried to the citadel with pace,
He then took the ladies, up to the highest place.
And in all directions they turned their lovely eyes,
They beheld Valencia and how the city lies,
And in another quarter they could perceive the sea,
They looked at the fertile meadows, and how great they be,
And at all things, whatever was now their estate,
They praised God with their hands, for a prize so good and great.

My Lord Cid was glad, and so were his men,
Now winter was over, because the March would come again.
And to the countries overseas it's my desire to tell,
Even to the King Yussuf in Morocco, who over there dwells.

The King of Morocco's heart, against Cid was full of rage.
"By force the man has entered into my heritage,
And gives thanks to no one except Jesus Christ therefor."
While saying, the King of Morocco gathered all his men of war.

With fifty times a thousand of arms, good men and stark,
They put on the ships and the army did embark,
To seek Cid Rodrigo in Valencia they went,
The ships came in; and straight away deployed their armament.

Where!
To Valencia that Cid had taken, the unbelievers pitched pavilions there.

With news of the chances, to my Lord Cid they came.
"Now thanks to the Creator and the Holy Father's name.
All the goods in my possession, I have them here with me,
I only just took Valencia, but I hold it for my fee;
On one side death, I cannot yield to it. Glory to God again,
And to Holy Mother Mary, that my wife and daughters came,
And are here with me. From overseas came my delight,
Never will I relinquish it, I will take the arms of fight,
My lady and my daughters will not see me fall but stand,
They will see how my men build houses here in a foreign land,
And how a livelihood is won, their eyes will see it well."
He took his wife and daughters up to the citadel.

They raised their eyes, and they saw men pitching tents everywhere,
"Cid, what is this? May the Lord still keep you in His care."

"Ha, my much honoured wife! Do not be troubled, trust."

"This wealth most great and wondrous, they gather here for us?"

"Yes, barely have you come, and they bring presents in this hour.
For your daughters too, who wait for marriage in the tower."

"To you Cid, and to God I give thanks again"

"My lady, in the palace or in the citadel remain.
When you see me in battle, do not fear at all for me.
By Saint Mary Mother's mercy, by God's charity,
You are here before me, my heart grows great within.
With God's help, this battle I certainly will win."

Now the pavilions were pitched, quickly the morning comes,
And furiously an atheist beat loudly on the drums.

"It is a great day," with a glad heart my Lord Cid said,
But his lady was so frightened, she almost lost her heart and head;
The ladies and his daughters were likewise all in fright,
Never had they heard such a sound a day in their whole life.

Immediately the great Cid, plucked his beard contemplating the raid.
"This will all be to your advantage, therefore do not be afraid,
When fifteen days are over, if God's will it be,
We will take those drums and show them to you, and you will see.
And then to Bishop Don Jerome they will be given;
They will be hung in Saint Mary's, Mother of the Lord who's in Heaven."

This was a most solemn vow that my Lord Cid had made,
The ladies were now merry and not so afraid.
Those Moors from Morocco, who now appear,
Rushed into the gardens and entered without fear.

The man on the outpost let the bell sound,
Cid Roy Diaz was ready with his company all around.
They went forth, from the city with their arms pointed well.
When they came to the Moriscos, on them swift fell.
They drove them from the gardens, such a sorry sight;
Out of the Moors, a full five hundred were slaughter in that fight.

Even to the pavilions the pursuers would not slack,
They had done so much, when they thought of turning back.
There Alvar Salvadorez, remained,
Then those that ate bread with him, returned to the Lord Cid again.
With his own eyes he observed it, they celebrated what they had done,
My Lord Cid was gladdened by the battle they had won.

"My knights we can do no more, listen to me:
It's a noble day, yet nobler tomorrow's battle will be.

My daughters wait for marriage, to God I give thanks again.
My lady along with them, in the palace where they remain.
When you see me in a battle, have no fear for me.
By Mother Mary's mercy, and God with his charity,
You are here before me, my heart grows great within.
With God and his help, any battle I certainly will win."

Arm yourselves. Bishop Don Jerome will take our confessions,

Saying mass for us here, we attack them tomorrow at eleven.
It will be in no other fashion, we will go defeat the foe,
In God's name and his Apostle's the good Saint James also.
It's better to fight than let them in the land to take our bread. "

"With a good will and gladly," in reply to him they said:

Minaya spoke: "for the need of battle grant me more horses and then,
From the side, when you charge I will fall on them.
On one side or the other my Lord we will stand our stead."

"With great good will," to him Cid said.

First came the morning, and then came the night,
That group of Christians did not delay to get ready for the fight.
Cockerels signalled the morning, at mass Don Jerome gave his chant,
Mass gives forgiveness, and in full to them did it grant:

"Who face to face will perish on this day, and face the fight within,
May Christ receive his spirit, and from his soul take away his sin.
Cid, Don Rodrigo, in good hour you hold the sword; to you I sang the mass this morning, and ask a favour too:
Allow me to strike the foremost, and first stroke of the war."
"To you it is granted," the Lord Cid swore.

Out through the Towers, fully armed away they went,
With Lord Cid, his men discussed all and then gave their

consent.
Some men they left behind them at the gates to watch and keep.
On the horse Bavieca sprang Lord Cid with a giant leap.
Rich accessories and reigns on that horse about,
With the standard from Valencia they swift rode out.

With Cid four thousand, plus or minus ten,
Came gladly to a battle against fifty thousand men.
Alvar Alvarez and Minaya on the other side prepared to strike,
It seemed good to the Creator, and they threw them into flight.
With the lance Cid battled hard, and with the sword as well,
So many Moors he slaughtered, that the numbers none could tell.
Down from his elbow, the blood of battle came,
Even against King Yussuf he took his aim.
He escaped from underneath the sword because his horse had good pace,
And took him to Cullera, an exceedingly mighty place.
However Cid of Vivar pursued them as they fled,
And a group of gallant men in his company swiftly sped.
He who in happy hour was born, from that pursuit turned back,
He was gladdened by the rewards they had taken from this attack.
Bavieca seems in good shape to him, from head to tail on that day,
In his hands remained the rewards of that battle and their prey.
Out of Fifty thousand in total, when it was finally counted,
A hundred and four escaped mounted.
My Lord Cid and his men searched the field around,
In gold and silver three thousand coins they found,

And the other rewards were theirs to be had,
My Lord Cid and his men were all exceedingly glad.
In the winning of this battle, God's grace to them was shown,
When the king of Morocco in his disguise was overthrown.
Cid left Alvar Fanez to count the dead and slain.
And then, with one hundred horses he entered Valencia again.
He rode without his helmet, his armour was disarrayed,
Through the town on Bavieca he galloped, with his hand upon the blade.
The ladies welcomed him well, as he entered through the gate,
My Lord Cid went before them, reining the horse to a sudden brake:

"Ladies, I bow before you, my name and fame,
Has grown, while you have held Valencia in the field I overcame.

This was our God's desire and all his Saints likewise,
Since you arrived, he gave us such a prize.
Look at the bloody sword and the horse with sweat like foam,
From the battle with Moriscos who in the battle were overthrown.
Pray to God now, that I may live a few years from this,
You will gain great honour, and men your hands will kiss."

He spoke as he dismounted, then stood for all to see,
When the ladies, his daughters and his wife of high degree,
Saw him get off, they kneeled before the Champion:
"It will be done, and may you live through many long years to come."

To the palace they returned, all much less difficult,
They rested on benches most exquisitely built:

"Lady Ximena, wife of mine, was it ever your view?
That these ladies you have brought here, would wait on you,
In marriage to my men I am eager to give them,
And to every lady for her share, two hundred coins along with them.
Men should know their good service, in the Kingdom of Spain.
With my maids here after at leisure they'll remain."
All there stood up together, and kissed his fingers straight,
The rejoicing in the palace was exceedingly great.

As my Lord Cid commanded, they quickly made their way,
Minaya Alvar was delighted, and offered no delay.
With his men to count the arms, tents and rich array,
A great store was discovered, taken from their prey.
But the richest of the treasure I will now to recite:
The tale of all the horses they could not take alright.
Richly adorned they wandered, but none would take a horse,
The Moors out of their provinces had gathered wealth of course.
Some of them were taken and given to the Champion,
Out of the best horses, his share was fifty one.
Cid had so many, but there were plenty more,
And rich pavilions, oh my god, what a store.

To Lord Cid and his men, the chance of war fell,
And the King of Morocco was the richest as well,
The pavilions were erected with golden tent-poles that bordered,
The field, My Lord Cid the great Champion ordered,

To take them down, no Christian should dare,
"Since to here from Morocco there has never been a tent so fair,
To Alfonso the Castilian I am eager to send the news;
That Cid has captured somewhat, then it will certainly be reviewed."

Loaded with mighty riches to Valencia they went home,
That very noble cleric, the Bishop Don Jerome,
With an excess of fighting he had with his own hands killed,
And was unable to number the Moors and how much blood spilled.
What came to him of the riches, was of great of worth.
My Lord Cid Don Rodrigo, in a happy hour was his birth,
Out of his fifth share of the rewards sent the tenth part,
To the Christians in Valencia, who were very glad of heart,
Because now excelling riches, horses and weapons they had,
Ximena and her daughters were all exceedingly glad,
And the other ladies, they,
Considered themselves as married, and my Lord Cid would not delay.

"Where are you brave Minaya? Come to me,
For your great share of riches, no gratitude I see.
Out of this fifth of all the winnings, I tell you clear and plain,
Take for your good pleasure, but let the rest remain.
And tomorrow in the morning you will certainly ride out,
With the horses of my portion that I captured in the rout,
With the saddles and the reigns, and the swords above,
For the sake of my lady and for the daughters that I love.
Since Alfonso sent the ladies away they were content,

These same two hundred horses to him you will present,
Of he who rules Valencia, the King no ill can say."

He asked Pero Vermudoz to join Manaya, and to go straight away.

The next day in the morning they departed with great speed,
And a full two hundred men along with them as they lead,
With greetings from Cid who was eager to kiss his hands alright,
Even after the battle where my Lord Cid had won the fight.

As a gift he sent to Alfonso two hundred horses or more:
"While I have breath within me, I will serve him evermore."

They left from Valencia, while the weather was quite fair,
They must watch well, over such great rewards that they bear.
And night and day they rushed onward, they gave themselves no rest,
The mountains that divide the clouds, they passed over the crest.
Along the way they asked the people, where was Alfonso's abode,
Over the mountains, over the rivers, over the hills they took the road.
And at length before Valladolid where,
The King was, Minaya and Pero Vermudoz sent news to him there.
A great reception of followers gave the King,
"My Lord Cid of Valencia sent us here to you with what we bring."

The King was glad, gladder than you could ever see,
He commanded all his men to ride forward hastily.

And along with the first of them, you could see King Alfonso go,
To him who in good hour was born with news to know.
The Men of Flesh now, waiting in that place to be,
That you can count Don Garcia as Cid's worst enemy.
From the news some were merry, and some were dejected,
They caught sight of his men, the one who was respected.
They feared it was an army, as no banner was assessed,
Straight away King Alfonso made a cross, across the chest.

Minaya and Pero Vermudoz came forward with haste of course,
They leaped from the saddle, they dismounted from the horse.
Before the King Alfonso they fell upon their knees,
They kissed the ground beneath him, and each of them said please:

"A favour King Alfonso, the great and glorious,
For my Lord Cid the Champion we embrace you as thus.
He considers himself your servant; and has you for his Lord,
He esteems the honour you gave him, of your own accord.
O King, a few days ago, in the fight he overcame,
The King of Morocco, Yussuf, as that is his name,
With fifty thousand men, from the field he drove away.
The prizes that he captured, were so great and best of all,
Much wealth and proportion to his followers did fall.
He sends two hundred horses and kisses your hands as well,

King Alfonso said: "I accept them gladly, and have something to tell,
To Cid who sent me such a gift, I send my thanks again,

I am glad I am to his liking, may he live a long life, and his men."

Count Don Garcia was distressed, angered was his heart within,
Also he moaned a little with ten other men of his kin:

"A marvel is this matter of Cid, how he grows his fame,
Now with the honour that he has we will all be put to shame,
Kings he overthrows lightly, and lightly gives horses,
And as if he found them dead; we are diminished by his forces."

Listen to what King Alfonso said about this score:
"Give thanks to the Creator and the Lord Saint Isidore,
For the two hundred horses that Cid to me has sent,
These shall serve me better in this my government.
To Minaya Alvar Fanez and Pero Vermudoz I say,
That onward you clothe your bodies in honourable array,
And as you require, take from me your battle-gear,
Such before Roy Diaz, in a good manner you shall appear.
Take then the gift I give you, out of these horses, three,
As it seems to my advisement, as my heart is telling me,
Out of all these adventures some good will come to light."

They kissed his hands and entered to take their rest that night.
In all things that they needed he told his men to serve them well,

More about two Heirs of Carrion I am eager to tell,
How secretly they counselled, what things should be their

cause:

"With my Lord Cid the high affairs go forward without pause,
Let us demand his daughters, so with them we may wed.
Our fortune and our honour will therefore be fed."

To the King Alfonso with their secret they proceeded.

"From our King and master, a blessing is needed,
A favour and your advice, along with your orders,
That you ask for us in marriage from Cid, with his daughters.
What an honour and profit we envisage."

For a full hour, the King pondered in thought over this image.

"If I order the good Champion, a wrong I must do him still,
Because he is good to me, I do not know if the match is to his will,
But we will do it anyway, since your pleasures ask."

For Alvar Fanez and Pero Vermudoz, the King gave a task.

He took them to the hall: "Now listen close,
Minaya and Pero Vermudoz. You know Cid serves you both;
The Champion has well earned his pardon from me,
And he has it. I will meet him, if his will shall be.
In discussion and other news from my court I will make it known,
Diego and Fernando, the Heirs of Carrion,
Are eager to wed his daughters, send the message well,

And I pray you seek the Champion with the news to tell.
It will be to his honour, great his fame will have grown,
When he becomes the father to the Heirs of Carrion."

Minaya spoke: (Pero Vermudoz's joy was very great)
"The execution of your desire we will undertake,
And Cid will do whatever he chooses."

"Say to Cid Roy Diaz the man that never loses,
That I will consult with him in the best place possible,
And there will be a boundary wherever he places an obstacle.
To my Lord Cid, I will show my favour plain."

To the King they said farewell, and then they were gone again.

Onward to Valencia they hastened with force,
When the good Champion had heard, he jumped upon his horse,
And came to meet them smiling, and strongly embraced the two.

"Minaya and Pero Vermudoz, you come back anew!
There are not many countries where two such brave men dwell,
From my Lord King Alfonso what news do you have to tell?
Is he content? Did he accept the gift from me?"

Minaya said, "In his soul and heart, he is content as content can be,
And his good will he sends to you furthermore. "

Cid said: "To the almighty Creator I have many thanks for."

Alfonso has made his pleasure known,
That Cid should give his daughters to the Heirs of Carrion.
He deemed it would make him glorious and cause his fame to grow,
And in all truth and honour even we would advise him so.
When my Lord Cid had heard it, the noble Champion,
A long time he passed in thought, until finally he was done.

"For this to Christ my master, I give my thanks again,
I was sent in to exile and my honour suffered a stain.
That which is mine I conquered, my endeavours high,
To God for the King's favour a thankful man am I,
And to them of Carrion, that they ask for my daughters too.
Minaya and Pero Vermudoz, what do you think you two?"

"Whatever is you will, that is all we will say."

Cid said: "The Heirs of Carrion, come from a great line don't they?
And they are exceedingly proud, and their favour is fair in the court,
Yet for such a marriage, my desire they have sought.
But since it is his pleasure, that is of worth to me,
Let us talk a little, but secret let us be.
May the Lord God in Heaven, advise and guide us best."

"Besides all we have told you, Alfonso has addressed:
That he would like to meet you in whatever place you choose,
He desires well to see you and honour you with the news.
So whatever suits you, it will be well agreed."

Cid said: "By saying this I am pleased indeed."

"Where would you like this meeting" said Minaya,
"consider well,
that the king desires it, there's nothing else to tell,"

But, wherever we might find him, we can seek him in his way,
As he is our King and Master, we have high respects to pay.
We will desire whatever good to him shall seem,
Close to the river Tagus, besides that noble stream.
If you my Lord desire, we will hold the meeting there."

He wrote the letters straight away and sealed them well and fair.

And then to two horsemen he gave the letters, done.
Whatever the King desires, is the will of the Champion.

To the much honoured King, the letters they present,
When he had finished reading, you could see his heart was content.

"To Cid who in good hour was born, my greetings I do send,
And let us hold the meeting when three weeks are at an end.
If I live, then no doubt I will wait for him in that place."

They did not delay, but rushed home to Cid with pace.

On both sides for the meeting, they got ready a device,
In Castile there was no such donkies that came without a price,
Not so many donkies, or strong horses swift to guide,
Or so many noble banners on the tall lances tied,

And embossed shields, with a gold and silver shine,
Robes, furs and Alexandrian cloth of satin woven fine.
And the King gave his orders, to send provisions there,
To the waters of the Tagus, for the meeting they prepare.
The King leads many troops, and Carrion's Heirs were glad.
Creating a new debt, but paid with what they had.
Because they thought they would gain great profit and increase it manifold,
And take whatever they desire, in goods of silver and of gold.
And now the King Alfonso got swiftly on his horse,
With counts and noblemen and servants in great force.
As for the Heirs of Carrion, great company they bring,
From Leon and from Galicia came so many people with the King.
Know well, the taxes of Castile, a never ending train,
And straight to the meeting they rode without a slackened rein.

In the city of Valencia, Lord Cid did not delay,
In regards to the meeting, he prepared himself for the day.
There were strong donkeys, men and concentrated forces,
A great store of armour, and many fleets of horses,
Many suits of armour, and many swords with all,
In apparel of all colours, clad both great and small.
Minaya Alvar Fanez and Pero Vermudoz there that night,
And Martin Munoz in Montemayor that held the rule of right,

And Martin Antolinez who in Burgos had his home,
And that most worthy cleric, the Bishop Don Jerome,
And with Alvar Salvadorez, Alvar Alvarez beside,
And likewise Nuno Gustoz a gallant knight up for the ride,
Also Galind Garciaz, from the Aragon's abode,
All of these to ride with the good Champion, got ready for

the road.

And the people in the palace prepared them all and one,
To Alvar Salvadorez and the man of Aragon,
Galind Garciaz, a command was given by the Champion,
That the heart and soul of Valencia they shall guard until their done.
And, moreover, all the others on their orders shall wait,
And my Lord Cid has ordered that they bar the castle gate.
And for no reason throw it open either by night or by day,
As his wife and his two daughters within will stay.
Those whom he loves best, along with the ladies that need protection still,
And so he ordered it, as any good Lord will,
That not a soul among them will venture from the tower,
Until Lord Cid returns to them, he who was born in good hour.

They left Valencia, forward they spurred along,
On their right were many horses, that were both swift and strong.
Cid had taken them, no man would have given up his horse,
And he rode onward to the meeting, all in due course.
In the light of day, he came before the King,
When they saw him coming, with open arms they bring.
With great worship to receive him, forward on to him they went,
When he had looked upon them, he was happy beyond extent.
He halted his companions, except his knights of dearest worth,
With fifteen of his men he jumped down to the earth.
Exactly as he who in good hour was born had willed that it should be,
Down to earth he went on the hand and knee.

And the grass of the meadow with his very lips he went,
And wept exceedingly, so great was his content.

To King Alfonso such respect he was prepared to show,
And there before his sovereign foot he showed him so.

As for King Alfonso, at heart it annoyed him much:

"Rise up! Rise up, on your feet, great Cid the Champion and touch,
My hand, not my feet, give my hand your embrace,
And if you will not do it, you will not have my grace."

But nonetheless the good Champion knelt on his bended knee:

"From my rightful master, a favour I wish to see,
And namely that your favour on me, you will care to bestow,
So that all the men around us, will hear and also know."

The King said: "Now that gladly and of good heart I will do;
And here I give you your pardon, and my favour I renew.
And you in my kingdom, a proper welcome I will extend."

My Lord Cid addressed him, after this wise man's talk was at an end:

"Mercy, Lord Alfonso, I will take what you have given.
I will go forward, for this I give my thanks to our God in Heaven,
And then to you, and to the men that around me stand."

And on the floor still kneeling, he kissed Afonso's hand.

To his feet he rose, and on the cheek placed a kiss,
The others in the presence were very pleased by this.
However, it annoyed Garci Ordonez and Alvar Diaz sore,
My Lord Cid spoke and uttered this saying furthermore:

"To our Father the Creator I offer thanks again,
That my Lord the King gave his pardon, and thanks to my men,
In the day and the night the Lord will esteem me higher,
And you will be my guest, my master, if it is your desire."

The King said: "Today in no way was that clearly in my sight,
That you would be here, but we came close last night,
Today, therefore, Cid Champion, you will remain my guest,
And tomorrow morning I will send you on your quest."

My Lord Cid kissed his hand, granting it should be so.
Then the Heirs of Carrion came, with their courtesy to show:

"Greetings Cid, you came forward in an hour which promised high.
And so far will we serve you as much as in our power lie."

"If the Creator grants it," Cid said.
My Lord Roy Diaz, who was born to go ahead,
To the King his master, he was a guest for that day and night,
The King held him in such grace, he could not let him leave his sight,
As Cid's beard grew so swiftly, long while the King did

stare,
At Cid they marvelled much, as many as were there.

And now the day was over, and upon them fell the night,
The next day in the morning the sun rose clear and bright.
Cid had requested from his men, a lot of meat for lunch,
With my Lord Cid the Champion, well content were the bunch,
All were very merry, and moreover of one mind,
That during three years together, so well they had not dined.

The next day in the morning, when at last the sun rose again,
Don Jerome the Bishop sang his song to them,
And when the mass had started, all gathered in one place,
And the King did not delay but began his speech with pace:

"Hear me now, counts and my loyal men so real,
To my Lord Cid the Champion I have to make an appeal.
The thing may prove of profit, I hope God grants it too,
Lady Sol and Lady Elvira, I ask their hands from you,
That you will in marriage, give them to the heirs of Carrion,
To me the match seems noble, and there much gain hangs upon.
They ask them from you, and to that end I add my own command,
On my side and yours, as many as around us stand,
My men and your men, let them therefor intercede,
Give them to us my Lord Cid, and God help give you speed."

Cid said: "My girls to marry, are hardly in that state,
As their days are not yet many, neither are their ages great.
As for the Heirs of Carrion, men have given them such

fame,
They match well with my daughters, and for them the same.
'I created my daughters, but you raised the two,
They and I for that reward, remain in debt to you.
Lady Sol and Lady Elvira, to you I do present,
To whomever you will give them, I will be content."

The King said: "My thanks to you and to all the court I own."
Upon their feet so swiftly were the Heirs of Carrion.
From him who in good hour was born, lightly they kissed the hands,
Before the King Alfonso they made exchange of bands.

King Alfonso spoke, like a man of gentle race:
"My thanks, so noble you are, but first to God for grace,
That for the Heirs of Carrion your daughters will be wed,
Lady Sol and Lady Elvira, in hand I have them led,
To Carrion's Heirs as partners those ladies I award,
I give away your daughters as brides of your own accord.
May it please God that you in full content may be.
Behold, the heirs of Carrion that now wait on you and me.
Let them go with you, please, because from here I must leave,
Three hundred coins of silver I give them for your ease,
To spend it on the marriage, or whatever else may please,
Since within high Valencia in your protection they will be.
The sons and the daughters as your children will be all four,
Whatever will be their pleasure, use it for them and more."

Cid received them from him, and to the King's hands he gave a kiss.

"My sovereign and my master, I think you well for this,
You will give away my daughters, as I will not do the

deed."

After the meeting was over they gave pledges and agreed.

That the next day in the morning, when the sun lit it's flame,
All persons at the meeting should return to from where they came.
Now both the fame and honour my Lord Cid had gained,
And many strong donkies and mighty horses tamed,
And fine and precious clothing, giving gifts he began,
To anyone who would take, and denied them to no man.
A full sixty horses, the Lord Cid did present,
To whoever was at the meeting and this made him well content.

Now they were eager to depart, as day was about to shed,
The King, took the Heirs of Carrion by the hand and led,
Them, in to the power of Cid the Champion,

"Here are your children; since now they are your sons,
From this day forward do with them as your heart accords.
May they serve you as their father, and keep you as their Lord."

"I thank you and accept, O King, the gift which you have given.
May you be well rewarded by our God who is in heaven.

Alvar Fanez said, "From you, my Lord, a favour I request,
I give to you my daughters to wed, in whatever way suits you best,
Choose one of my girls to give away, who else in your place could stand,
Since you have them, I will never give them to anyone with

my own hand.
To the Heirs, no satisfaction will be denied."

"Look here Alvar Fanez," the mighty King replied.

"Give them to heirs, as if they came straight from me,
Like it was I who offered them, to cure my poverty,
And in to the future, their sponsor you will be,
And whenever you return, tell all the truth to me.
Have faith! My Lord, I will be content indeed."

To all this with due caution, you should know that they agreed.

"Ha! King, my Lord Alfonso, much honoured, for a sign,
Of the meeting that we held here, please take a gift of mine.
I bring you thirty donkies that are accessorised with rich apparel,
And thirty more war-horses, each with a noble saddle.
Take them and I will kiss your hand." King Alfonso said:

"Deep in your debt you have me, your gift I will accept,
Which you, the Creator and all his saints accord,
For the kindness you have shown me you will gain a fair reward.
Oh my Lord Cid Roy Diaz, you gave an honour so high.
You have earned my service, and well content am I.
May you reap from me some harvest, when my life is at an end,
Now I must leave, from this meeting we attend.
Praise God in Heaven! Grant our agreement is well kept."

Cid mounted Bavieca, on to his horse he leapt.

"Here before my King Alfonso I say it openly,

Who wants to attend the marriage or seeks a gift from me,
Let him come with me, his profit will be great, as I conceive."

Now from his Lord Alfonso, Lord Cid took his leave.

His company he no longer needed, he departed from him straight,
Now you would see many knights enough to fill a large estate.
Upon leaving King Alfonso, his hands he did kiss:

"Let it be your will, and God please grant us this,
Cid of great Valencia, now we will march away,
To see the Heirs of Carrion upon their wedding day,
With Lady Sol and Lady Elvira, who Cid's daughters be."

Upon this the King was satisfied, and gave them liberty.

The King's group of men diminished, and in to Cid's they poured,
A great company of people now marched with Cid my Lord.

They rode straight to Valencia following the star as it was so high.
On Diego and Fernando he asked them keep an eye.
Muno Gustoz and Pero Vermudoz they had commanded fair,
In all of Lord Cid's following there was not a better pair.
As for the heirs of Carrion, to discover their ways and find,
Ansuor Gonzalez joined them and followed them from behind,
Loose-tongued, and untrustworthy, and in other things well

known,
They showered many honours on the Heirs of Carrion.

In the distance they saw Valencia, that my Lord Cid had taken,
When they looked at the city they were exceedingly impatient.

Muno Gustoz and Don Pero said: "Straightway take them to a good room,
Do not delay with them, execute my order soon.
When the morning comes, and the sun rises bright,
Have Lady Sol and Lady Elvira, their brides, within their sight."

Cid Champion entered his castle, after giving his orders,
Home of Lady Ximena, she and her daughters.

"Best Champion to ever hold the sword, everyone hopes he stays;
May the eyes of our faces get to see you many days."

"I am home, much honoured wife, by the Creator's grace,
And sons-in-law I bring you, now our fame will grow with pace.
I have married you well my daughters, so thank me for it well."

Kissing his hands, his wife and his daughters fell.

And likewise all the ladies in the home did.

"Thanks to the Creator and to you, fair-bearded Cid,

What a thing you have achieved, it is well done indeed,
In all your days your daughters will never be in need."

"When you give us in marriage, great wealth to us will fall."

"Wife of mine, Lady Ximena, praise God who made us all.
Lady Sol and Lady Elvira, my girls to you I say,
From your marriage, you honour will increase in every way.
But this I did not begin, the truth now understand,
My Lord Alfonso sought you and imposed his demand.
With such firm will, I did not know how to deny the thing.
And I put you both, my daughters, in the keeping of the King.
Know that he gave your hands to wed, and that I am not the man."

To beautify the palace, one and all began.

Much drapery was displayed, on the floor and on the walls,
Much purple and interwoven silk, covering the stalls.

It would have pleased you, if you could be there to eat,
On a seat or on your feet. Rapidly his knights gathered round to meet.
And the Heirs of Carrion, at that time had sent,
For their horses, they got on and onward to the palace they went.
Their apparel all fine, only the best,
They arrived properly, God! in what a humble dress!
Cid and all his men received them when they came,
They bowed their heads before him; they bowed before his Dame,
To take their seats among them, straight away they strode,

My Lord Cid and all his men had wisdom and this they clearly showed.
A speech from Cid, in quiet all expect,
And suddenly the noble Champion stood up erect:

"Since such a good deed is coming, why do we delay here?
Come here Alvar Fanez, whom I cherish and hold dear.
My daughters, look at them, your hands I place them within,
Make it known, so as to perform what I swore to the King.
To fail in our agreement is in no way my intent,.
To the Heirs of Carrion, their brides, with your hand present.
Let them have my blessing and speed the wedding through."

To him Minaya replied: "This I will gladly do."

The ladies rose, and he placed them into Minaya's care.
To the Carrion's Heirs, Minaya stood to declare:

"Listen brothers! And shortly you will see!
By the hand of King Alfonso, who has placed this charge on me,
I give to you these ladies that are both of noble blood,
That to be your wives you take them gladly, and shower them with love."

And with a will so gladly to take their brides they came,
They kissed the hands straight away of Lord Cid and his Dame.
They exited the palace, with all these things complete,
And then to Saint Mary's in haste they moved swiftly on their feet.
Bishop Jerome requested his garments, someone quickly

went to search,
For them, he dressed, and he stood at the doorway of the church.
He then given them his blessing, and chanted mass of course,
When the left the church they went with speed, each to get their horse.

They hastened from Valencia forward along the sandy shore,
God! Cid and his companions, carried many arms of war!
He born in happy hour, changed his horse three times,
With what he saw my Lord Cid was well content in his mind.
Because the two heirs of Carrion have on their horses bestowed,
The ladies to Valencia, then home again they rode.
All considered it stunning, the wedding that they had,
Cid set up seven posts, to watch them, the men were glad.

Before they went to dinner, the seven watched as closely as they could,
A full fifteen days together, during the wedding stood.
The fifteen days almost done; homeward the men ride,
With my Lord Cid Don Rodrigo who fought for the good side.
Donkies and horses and the battle-chargers swift,
Of animals alone a hundred was granted as a gift,
Cloaks and dress of other sorts, a great store,
And wealth in money, abundance furthermore.

As the men of Lord Cid, had been fully paid,
For their part, bridal keepsakes upon the guests they gave.
He came into great possession of wealth, he who endured the pain,

And wealthy he left the wedding to return to Castile again.
None of these guests, together were about to ride away,
Unless to Roy Diaz, their respects they pay,
And likewise to the ladies, and his men of high descent,
My Lord Cid and his men they left in high content.
They said much in honour of them, as was indeed their due.
Diego and Fernando were also merry too.
Count Don Gonzalo took them to be his children too.
And now the guests returning homeward to Castile anew.

Cid and his two sons-in-law in Valencia were to stay,
There dwelt the Heirs until two years passed away.
It was a mighty welcome in that city that they had,
Cid and all his men were all extremely glad.
Saint Mary and our Father, may it please them to consent,
That Cid and he who formed the wedding be content.

POEM 3

THE WOOD OF CORPES

Cid stayed in Valencia with all his men beside,
With him the Heirs of Carrion his sons-in-law abide.
Upon his couch to sleep, laid the good Champion,
There fell a hard occasion, a thing they had to overcome.
From his cage came a lion, his shackles he released,
All men throughout the palace were in mighty fear to say the least.

'By the side of the Champion his men made their fear so plain,
Around his couch they gathered, and beside their Lord remain.
As for Fernando Gonzalez the Heir of Carrion,
He saw no place to hide in; in the tower there was none.
Beneath the seat he crouched, so mighty was his dread,
And Diego Gonzalez out through the doorway fled,
Crying aloud: "God, Carrion no more shall I behold."
Inside a wine-press timber he hid in fear untold.

From there he brought back a cloak covered in dirt and muck,
With that Cid woke from sleep, and really he was struck,
He saw his good men round his couch, and observing them.

He said: "What is it that happened? What is this my men?"

"Worthy Lord! The lion gave us a fearful fright."
Cid leaned on his elbow, on his feet he leaped upright.
He flung his cloak on his shoulders, straight for the beast he

made,
When the lion saw him coming, it deeply was afraid.
In front of Cid, cowering, he was put in check,
My Lord Cid Don Rodrigo then took him by the neck.
He dragged him and threw him in a rage,
All that observed were amazed, as the lion landed in the cage.

Through the palace they returned to the hall,
To his sons Cid wanted to ask the question, but could not find them at all.
Though they shouted for them loudly, it was to no avail,
And when at last they found them, their checks were really pale!
So much humour was in the palace, which you never saw before,
But to make fun of them was forbidden by Cid as if it were a law.
Many took them to be cowards, from what both had shown,
Sorely grieved at what happened, were the heirs of Carrion.

From such an affair, truly they felt shame,
Then an attacker from Morocco to besiege Valencia came.
Their camp was within a quarter mile, which they enriched,
For fifty thousand men, with the pavilions they had pitched.
It was the King Bucar, if his stories you've heard anyone tell,
For Lord Cid and all his men, it pleased them very well.

Because by the Lord's favour their gain should grow some more,
But at present the Heirs of Carrion at heart were very sore.
Because they saw the Moriscos, camped within the many tents,
Which they did not like, at this, the brothers instantly went.

"We should keep in mind our profit, for a loss we have no care,
And now within this battle we have to do our share."

"Such a thing would keep us from seeing Carrion again.
Widows will be the daughters of our good Lord Champion."

But Munoz Gustoz noticed, how in secret they conferred.
To Cid Champion he came with the tale of what he heard:

"The two Heirs your sons-in-law, their courage is so strong,
Because they will go to battle, for Carrion they long.
As God cherishes and keeps them, go tell them to have good heart,
That their peace they do not delay, neither in battle should it part.
But with that we will conquer, and God will be our guide."

My Lord Cid Don Rodrigo had a smile very wide.

"My sons, the Heirs of Carrion. God have you in his care.
In your arms rest my daughters, that as the sun are fair.
And as I yearn for battle, and like you of Carrion have shown,
In secluded Valencia, your heart's desire will be known!
Because as for the Moriscos, them well enough I know,
And by the grace of the Creator I have courage to overthrow."

While they spoke, the King Bucar had commanded Cid to release,
Valencia, and go his way in peace.

Otherwise Bucar would take payment for all that Cid had done,
In the city. Cid said to him who gave the message: "Go to Bucar, that son, of an enemy, that before three days are past,
I will give him everything he asks."

Cid ordered his men to take their weapons, and march against the Moors,
The Heirs of Carrion on that occasion were not to be found indoors.
After Cid had called his men to battle, Don Fernando, an Heir,
Went forward to attack a Moor called Aladraf, who was not unaware.
The Moor, when he saw Don Fernando, came forward to attack,
Upon this the Heir of Carrion, being overcome with fear fell flat,
Wheeling his horse around, and then fled before him,
He did not dare to await the Moor, and wished it was morning.

When Pero Vermudoz, standing nearby saw this, he attacked the Moor, Fought with him and killed him, then went to find Fernando for sure.

He said to Fernando, "take this horse and tell them you killed the Moor,
I will be your witness, ok, I have opened the door"

And he replied: "Don Pero Vermudoz, I thank you greatly for this,
You have saved my honour, your hands I do kiss.
May I see the time when your favour will be returned again,

For all that you deserve". The pair turned back toward the men.

Don Pero acted as the witness to Fernando's brag and lie,
Which Cid and all his men were gladdened so much by.

"If God our Father wills it, in Heaven where they could dwell,
My sons-in-law in battle, he would both acquit them well."

As they spoke, the advance of armies now began,
In the Moorish group resounded the sound of drums, part of their plan.
Among the Christians, this was a marvel to some,
Because never had they heard it, marching as they come.

Diego and Fernando were in great fear of the brawl,
If it were their free will, they would not have come at all.
Listen to he who was born in a happy hour very clear:

"Don Pero Vermudoz, who to me is very dear,
Diego and Fernando, keep them well for me,
Because in my eyes, my sons-in-law are dear exceedingly.
With God's help the Moriscos will hold the field no more."

"In the name of every charity I will tell you plain,
To be their keeper I never will remain.
To me they matter little, let someone else keep them if they like,
With my men around me against the enemy I will strike.
Then you can aid me lightly, if peril should arise."

Minaya Alvar Fanez then came to him likewise.

"Oh, Cid, listen, oh faithful Champion, for sure!

In this battle, God himself will wage the war,
And He will direct your steps, in order for you to share,
Wherever you deem it best, for us to attack them there.
Each man must do his duty, grab the swords and let us thrust,
On God and on our fortune, hangs our trust."

Lord Cid said: "Then please do not delay here even for a while."

Don Jerome the Bishop who was armed in gallant style,
Stopped before the Champion, as he walked along the aisle.

"Lord Cid, I sought you as I have something to say,
The Mass of holy Trinity I sang for you today,
For this cause, from my own village, I left to seek you,
And since beating the Moors, I am delighted by what we do.
And I am eager to honour both my land and my hand,
In the forefront of the battle it is my desire to stand.
Crosses on my armour, and inscribed on my shield.
If it is God's pleasure, I am eager to be on the field.
That so at last my spirit, in perfect peace may be,
And you may be, my Lord Cid, content with me.
If you do not offer me this honour, from your side I will retire."

The Lord Cid gave his answer: "I am pleased with you desire.
Go make a trail of Moors wherever they are in sight,
For all of us to see, how a Vicar fights a fight."

And Don Jerome the Bishop went quickly on his way,
Straight out of the encampment, onward toward the fray.

With his good luck and God's who loved him well,
At the first stroke he delivered, in front of him two Moors fell.
But now his lance was broken, he placed his hand upon the blade.
In the Name of God! What a fair fight he made!
Two with their lances, and others with swords, five of them he slew,
So many Moors around him, and closely they drew.
They did not pierce his armour, though they gave him strokes with power,
He beheld the Bishop, who was born in happy hour.

Raising his shield, with it, the battle-spear he placed along,
He mounted Bavieca, the well-paced horse and strong.
He went to go against them, with all his soul and heart,
The highest ranks of battle, Lord Cid never could depart.
He struck down seven Moors, five of them he laid slain,
God was well pleased, the battle was granted for him to gain.
My Lord Cid and his men, in hot pursuit they went,
You could have seen the stakes uptorn, any many broken tents.
All the ten-poles falling, that were placed so well and deep,
From the tents, my Lord Cid's men drove King Bucar's men like sheep.

Out of the tents they drove them; and followed them with pace,
Many arms, and so much armour, had you ever seen give chase.
Many Moors heads with helmets, in the battle had fallen low,
And many rider-less horses that galloped to and fro.
For seven miles together they pursued and gave them fight,

As he followed King Bucar, Cid my Lord did right:

"Turn here Bucar, you have come from a land oversea,
Cid whose beard is mighty you meet with presently.
Let us greet, and in friendship let each to each be bound."

To Cid, Bucar answered: "Such a friendship God confounds.
A sword in your hand you hold, and you chase me hastily,
It seems you are eager to try that blade on me.
For my horse to fall and stumble, that's something you won't see,
You will never overtake us, as we ride into the sea."

My Lord Cid answered: "In truth, that promise you cannot keep."

Bucar had a good horse, that sprang off with a leap.
But Cid's Bavieca gained ground upon him fast,
Three meters from the water he caught Bucar at last.
He raised his sword so high, and gave a great strike,
On his head so hard, with all of his might.
He cut straight through the helmet, sliced it straight in two,
Down to the belt of the King, the sword all the way went through.
Bucar the King from overseas, Cid had overthrown,
Worth over a thousand gold coins, was the great sword Tizon,
That he took, 'It was a marvellous victory and one so great,
From this Lord Cid gained honour, and all on him who wait.

And now with all they won, homeward again they wheeled,
But before they left, meticulously they looted all the field.
With the one and only, back they went again,

My Lord Cid Roy Diaz, the famous Champion.
With two swords he greatly cherished, from the carnage that he took,
His head cap was wrinkled, on his face was a look,
Of pride. A little ruffled was the cap on his hair,
On every side his men came running to him there.
My Lord Cid observed it, and it pleased his eye,
So as he looked before him, he raised his eyes so high.
He saw Diego and Fernando, that near to him drew,
For Count Don Gonzalo the children were his too.

My Lord Cid smiled beautifully, what a sight to see.

"Come here, my sons-in-law, you are both dear to me.
I know that with the fighting you are well content,
To Carrion the news that concerns you will be sent.
How by us King Bucar, to his defeat was thrust,
As sure as to the Lord God and all his saints I trust.
With the defeat of the enemy we can all be satisfied,
Minaya Alvar Fanez now came to his side.

His shield had been hacked by swords, which was on his neck he wore,
The strokes of many lances had scarred it furthermore.
Those that struck those strokes, had reaped no gain,
Down his elbow a bloodstream, more than twenty had he slain.

"To God and to the Father how highly we must praise,
And to Cid who was born in good hour a toast to you I raise.
You killed King Bucar, and so you won the day,
For you and for your men, we should prey.

And as for your sons-in-law they have been proved aright,
They got their fill of Moorish war upon the field of fight."

My Lord Cid said in answer: "Therefore I am very glad,
Since they have been proven, in high esteem they should be had."

In honesty he said it, but it was a joke they thought.
To Valencia, the winnings, they gathered and they brought.
My Lord Cid was merry and so were his men with him there,
Six hundred coins of silver were proportioned to his share.

The sons-in-law of Cid, when they had taken away,
Their war-prize and it was in their hands, they,
Took care, that no decreased in their time was made,
In the city of Valencia they were splendidly arrayed.
Eating well, and wearing good clothing and lovely capes of fur,
Cid and all his men, exceedingly glad they were.

I was a great day in the palace of Cid the Champion,
When he had killed King Bucar, and on the field of war they won.
He raised his hand, he plucked his beard: "To Christ this glory be,
Who is the Lord of all the Earth, and all my desires see.
That with me in the battle, my two sons attacked the foe,
Good news about them, off to Carrion will go,
How greatly they are honoured, and what renown they gain."

Such greats rewards after the battle, Cid took from the campaign.
Part belongs to them, in their safety kept aside,

My Lord Cid gave new orders, that all they keep inside,
To the men of that conquest, his true share they should split,
After for my Lord Cid, they segregate a fifth of it.
And they did just that, being prudent all and one,
For his fifth, six hundred horses my Lord Cid had won.
And there were many camels and, moreover, donkies as well,
So many were there, that their number none could tell.

All of this as captured by the great Champion:

"Now to God we give this glory, to the father and the son.
Before I was in poverty and have grown rich and great,
Because now I have possessions, gold, honour, and estate.
And the two Heirs of Carrion who I treat as my sons,
And since it is God's pleasure in every battle I have won.
The Moors now dread the Christians, shaking in great fear,
All over in Morocco, and any over here.
Where all men are in terror, do I descend?
Or at night? That I in no way I intend.
I will not go to seek them, in Valencia I will stay,
By God's aid, to me their tribute they will render up and pay.
To me or to my men, they will pay the money down."

Such a state of joy there was in Valencia and the town.
That rose all the taxes, of Cid the Champion,
That with God's will, the war they had won.
Likewise of both his sons-in-law excelling was the joy,
As each of them won five thousand coins to enjoy.
They deemed it wealthy, both the Heirs of Carrion,
And along with the others, to the palace they went on.
With my Lord Cid the Bishop Don Jerome stood on the right,

And on the left the good Alvar Fanez, one courageous knight,
In the house of Cid, there were many more,
Great praise was given when the heirs of Carrion entered the door.

When they came in the Champion was merry and of good cheer:

"My sons-in-law, my faithful wife and dear,
Lady Sol and Elvira, my daughters, the pair,
Now may they serve you, and entertain you there.
Glory to Saint Mary, Mother of our Lord! In God's name!
From these your marriages you will win abundant fame.
To the land of Carrion, great news will be sped."

Then the Heir Fernando spoke when all these words were said:

"Glory to the Creator, and to noble Cid,
We have so many riches thanks to everything you did.
Through you we have much honour, and we have fought for you,
We conquered the Moriscos in the battle, then we overthrew,
King Bucar, the proven traitor, so we pray that you have care,
Now for some other matters, well matched to our affair."

Cid's men spoke to each other, smiling all around,
About who fought most fiercely, and who wasn't to be found.

Diego and Fernando were not found among such men,
There was so much commotion, all were laughing at them.

Day and night together they mocked the Heirs again,
Until a very evil conversation took place between them.
Of course they are brothers, toward each other they turn,

"To the things that they have said, let us have no concern.
Let us return to Carrion, it's been such an overlong wait,
The riches we have gathered are excellent and great.
We cannot hope to spend them, over the course of our lives".

"From Cid the Champion let us demand our wives,
Let us say that we will take them to the lands of Carrion,
To them, the place where they are heiresses is yet to be shown.
We will take them from Valencia, away from the Champion and his reach,
And then along the journey we will work our will on each.
Here the matter of the lion, for the insult and scorn,
Turned in to our discomfort, two heirs who are Carrion born.
We will hold with us treasure, priceless piece we have a fair stock,
The daughters of the Champion, will be ours to mock.
We will be rich men always, who possess such valiant things,
And fit to marry daughters of emperors or kings.
The Counts of Carrion, by virtue of our birth,
The Champion and his daughters we will mock their lowly worth.
The matter of the lion, they throw at us in disdain."

When they had decided this the two returned again,
When they entered, there was silence in the Court:

"Cid the Champion, may our God always offer you strong support,
I hope it pleases Lady Ximena, but first seems good to you,
And Minaya Alvar Fanez and all men here too.
Give us our wives, by marriage they are ours indeed,
And to our lands in carrion those ladies we will lead.
The lands we offer them are given as their bridal right,
All of our possessions, your daughters will have sight,
And the children to be born, will also have their share."

Cid my Lord the Champion could see no insult there:

"I will give you my daughters and my wealth, some.
You give them possession, of the lands in Carrion,
Three thousands coins of silver, to my girls belong,
I will give donkies and horses, both excellent and strong,
And great horses of battle, swift and of mighty,
And cloth and silk garments with gold woven tightly.
Colada and Tizon the swords I give likewise,
You know full well, I got them in very gallant guise.
You are my sons, you I give my daughters to,
My very heart's blood you carry home with you.
In Leon and in Galicia and Castile let all men hear,
How I sent my sons-in-law with such abundant gear.
Serve well my daughters, as well as can be,
And if you serve them well, more riches come from me."

The heirs of Carrion, had not been mistaken,
The daughters of Cid were given, and then taken.
And they pretended to care, as Cid's orders went,
That it was to their heart's desire, and they were content.
Then Carrion's heirs commanded that the bags be loaded by the gate,
To leave for Carrion, business was pressing great.
They took all the weapons and the men galloped strong,

Because they must escort the daughters of Cid to speed along.
To the lands of Carrion, to mount, as all men prepare,
Farewell the men were saying, to the two sisters there,
Lady Sol and Lady Elvira, kneeled before Cid to plead:

"A favour, so may God keep you safe, O father, we need.
You produced us, and our mother brought us forth in pain,
Our liege-Lord and our lady, in front of us you both stand here in Spain.
Now to the lands of Carrion, to send us is your will,
It is our duty, to follow your commandments and fulfil.
And so we both together, ask this favour from you,
That in the lands of Carrion, we always hear what's new."

My Lord Cid held them, and he kissed the two,
After he had done this, their mother did so too.

"Go, daughters! From the creators of you, take care,
Mine and your father's blessing you take with you there.
Go, where you will live in Carrion and dwell,
I have, to my thinking, married you very well."
The hands of their father and their mother both kissed,
Letting them know, they will surely be missed.

My Lord Cid and the others prepared them to ride,
With armour and with horses and with banners of pride.
From Valencia to Carrion, the Heirs were departing then,
They left with the ladies and a large group of men.
Through the meadow of Valencia forward, on the way they went,
Cid and all his army were very well content.
However he knew, in signs and had seen it plain,

That these marriages in no way could stand without a stain.
But since the two are married, he could not regret it too.

"My nephew Felez Munoz, come to me, where are you?
You are my daughters' cousin, in soul and in heart,
With them to Carrion I command you to depart.
You will see, what land my sons-in-law are giving,
And will return to give me the news of how my daughters are living."

Felez Munoz said: "In my heart and soul that duty I guarantee."

Minaya Alvar Fanez came before Cid and said: "listen to me,
Back to the town of Valencia, Oh Cid, let us go;
Because if our God and Father the Creator's wills it so,
We will be in the Carrion's lands, to visit your daughters,
For Lady Sol and Lady Elvira, let God give his orders.
Perhaps such things you will accomplish and make us glad."

The sons-in-law answered: "Leave it to God to decide what's to be had."

They cried so much at parting, the daughter's tears were sore,
And for the knights of Cid Champion even more.

"You, cousin, Felez Munoz, listen to this aright,
You will go by Molina, and there sleep only one night,
And greet the fair the Morisco Avengalvon my friend;
So he, a fair reception to my sons-in-law will extend.
Tell him I send my daughters to the lands of Carrion,
In all their needs his courtesy and favour will be shown.

Let him accompany them to Medina, out of the love he has for me,
For all that he does for them I will give him a rich fee. "

They parted then, like when a nail out of the flesh is torn,
He turned back to Valencia he who in happy hour was born.
And now the Heirs of Carrion were riding fair,
To Saint Mary of Alvarrazin, their stopping-place was there.

Then the Heirs of Carrion rushed furiously away,
To Molina with the Moor Avengalvon in one day.
When he heard, the Morisco in his heart was content,
And forward with great delight to welcome them he went.
Ah, God! How well he served the whole lot!
The next day in the morning upon the horse he got.
And commanded two hundred horsemen to escort them for the ride,
They crossed the mountains of Luzon, (as they are signified),
And the Vale of Arbujunoj to Jalon they came,
The place where they found lodging, Ansarera was its name.

To the daughters of Cid, fair presents the Moor gave,
And next to them the Heirs of Carrion stood beside looking brave.
Out of the love he had for the Champion, all this for them he did,
They were looking at the riches, the Moor willed to give.

And then together, more justice the brothers wanted to pervert,

"Since the daughters of the Champion we will shortly

desert,
If we put to death Avengalvon the Moor,
The treasure he possesses for ourselves we will secure.
Together with our wealth in Carrion those goods we will maintain,
And never will Cid Champion be able to place on us this stain."

While they of Carrion this shame, plotted each with each,
In the middle of it a Moor overheard them, that understood Latin speech.
He kept no secret, with it to Avengalvon he ran:

"You are my Lord, be wary of these persons they have a plan.
I heard the heirs of Carrion plotting your death when they can."

This same Avengalvon the Moor, was a such a gallant man,
He got straight away on horseback, with two hundred men,
He brandished his weapons high, as he came before them.
And the two Heirs, with what he said were not very pleased:

"If it wasn't for my Lord Cid of Vivar, I would not leave,
I would do deeds against you, which through the whole world would ring,
And then to the true Champion his daughters I would bring.
And Carrion, you would never enter again from that day.
What I have done for you! Heirs of Carrion, what do you say?
Without deceit I served you, and my death you plot,
Such wicked men and traitors I will leave you on the spot.
Lady Sol and Elvira, with your permission I will go,
As these men of Carrion, I rate their worth very low.

God will it and command it, who is Lord of all to see,
That the Champion from this match has as much joy as can be."

That was all Moor had told them, he turned his back on them there,
When he crossed over the Jalon, his weapon he waved in air,
He returned to Molina, like a man of prudent heart,
And now from Ansarera to Carrion the Heirs depart.

They began thereafter to travel day and night,
And they let Atienza on the left, a descended from a height.
The forest of Miedes, then they overpassed,
And on through Montes Carlos they pushed onward moving fast.
And then passed Griza on the left, that Alamos was around,
Where in the caves of Elpha, he imprisoned underground.
And they left San Estevan, on their right that lay afar,
Within the woods of Corpes, the Heirs of Carrion are.
And the high hills are wooded, to the clouds the branches sweep,
And savage are the creatures, that all around them creep.
And there upon a grove, with a clear spring of light,
The Heirs of Carrion asked that their tent be pitched that night.
And with their men around them, that night they lay at rest,
With their wives clasped to their chest, their affection they protest,
But they could not feel it, then the sun raised in the East,
They packed the goods on the back of every beast.
Where they at night found lodging, now others placed the tent,
The people of their household, far on before them went.
So from the two Heirs of Carrion, a new commandment

ran,
That none should liger behind, not a woman or a man.
But Lady Sol and Elvira, their wives to delay it still,
Wanted to linger with whoever it was their pleasure to their fill.
The others had departed, just the four were left alone,
Great evil had been plotted by the Heirs of Carrion.

"Lady Sol and Elvira, you may take this for true:

Here in the desert a mock will be made of you.
Today is our departure, we will leave you here behind,
And in the lands of Carrion no portion you will find.
Let anyone take the news to Cid Champion,
And here, the matter of the lion, our revenge we have done.
Their coats and their jewellery, from the ladies they whipped,
In their shirts and their tunics they left the ladies stripped.
After they had observed it, Lady Sol spoke:

"Don Diego, Don Fernando, this must be a joke.
You have two swords with you, that for their strength are known,
One they call Colada, the other is Tizon.
Strike off our heads together, and martyrs we will die,
The Moriscos and the Christians against this deed will cry.
It's not to our deserving, that we should suffer thus,
Such an evil example, that you make of us.
Our humiliation, if you punish us, you consent,
Many men will bring charges against you in parliament."

It was to no profit, no matter how much they cried,
And now the Heirs of Carrion, had them on the floor tied.
With the buckled belts they beat them in fashion never seen,

And beyond sense was their anguish, they hit them so keen.
Once they had finished and wounded the bodies of the two,
Upon the tunics the clear blood trickled through.
In their very hearts the ladies felt agony,
What an unfair fortune, if God's will it had to be,
Appearing before them was Cid the Champion,
Powerless were the ladies, and the brothers were not done.

Taking it in turns, and on the tunics throughout the blood did sprout,
The beating of the two ladies tired the brothers out.

Which man could hit harder, battled each with each,
Lady Sol and Elvira no longer had power of speech.
Within the wood of Corpes, for dead they left the pair,
Taking their coats and jewellery leaving them bare.
In their shirts and tunics, fainting, they left them there behind,
Prey for every wild-animal and beast of every kind.

Leaving them for dead, barely living, but still with good cheer,
Praying sincerely, for Cid, Roy Diaz, to appear.

The Heirs of Carrion for dead have left them there arrayed,
One man to another other sang each other's praise.
As they continued on their journey through the wood:

"For the question of our marriage we have made our vengeance good.
How regretful, to be our wives we should, not have taken them,
Because as wedded wives they were unfit for us men.
And for the insult of the lion, vengeance has been served."

Each other's praises, the Heirs of Carrion preserved.
But Felez Munoz, I will tell the tale once again,
Was nephew to Cid the Champion.

They had told him to ride onward, but he was not well content,
And his heart burned within him as along the road he went.

Straight away from all the others, to the side to withdraw,
Felez Munoz entered into a thick-overgrown straw.
Until the passing of his cousins could be plainly perceived,
He was oblivious to what the Heirs of Carrion had achieved.
Then he saw them coming, and wanted to hear what they say,
But they did not see him, and had not thought of him that day.

He would not have escaped death, if on him they laid an eye,
Luckily the two Heirs rode onward, quite fast as they went by.
On their trail, Felez Munoz turned back again.
He came across his cousins, and this is what happened then.
Crying "Oh my cousins!" he straight rushed forward,
By the reins, the horse he tethered, and went to them afterward.

"Lady Sol and Elvira, cousins of mine – how could this be?
The two Heirs of Carrion have done this disgracefully.
Please God, for this dealing may they receive a shameful gain."

And straight away he stirred them in to life again,
From his heart the very fabric inside was torn.

"Oh my cousins Lady Elvira, Lady Sol," he cried as if to mourn.
"For the love of God stay awake, until the evening-hour,
Or else in this wood our bodies the savage beasts will devour. "

In Lady Sol and Lady Elvira fresh life began to rise,
And they looked at Felez Munoz when at last they opened their eyes:

"For the love of God my cousins, take courage, recoup.
From the time the Heirs of Carrion notice me missing from their group,
With utmost speed they will hunt me low and high,
And if God will not help us, in this place we must die."

To him Lady Sol spoke in bitter agony:

"The Champion, our father, does not deserve this tragedy.
My cousin please give us water, and may God help you too."

A hat from Valencia Felez Munoz had, fine and new,
Inside he had the water, which his cousins used,
To drink as much as they need, as they were sorely bruised.
Until they rose up, most sincerely he begged them and implored,
He comforted them and uplifted them until they were restored.
He took the two and quickly set them on a horse again,
He wrapped them in his clothing, he took the charger's rein
And on they sped, through Corpes Wood they took their way,
They went through the entire forest between night and day.

At the waters of Duero, and at the last they find,
Lady Urraca's tower, where he had left them behind.
And then to Saint Stephen's, they hurried,
He found Diego Tellez, Alvar Fanez' servant, who looked worried.
When he had heard the news, his heart felt great sorrow,
He gave animals of burden and garments to borrow.
He went to welcome Lady Elvira and Lady Sol,
He lodged there in Saint Stephen's, where great honour they show.
To those ladies, in Saint Stephen's very gentle were the men,
When they had heard the news their hearts were sorry for them.
To Cid's daughters abundant tributes were revealed,
The ladies remained there, until the time when they were healed.

Loud they sang each other's praises those Heirs of Carrion,
And the news of their deeds, through all the lands became known.
The good King Don Alfonso's heart in grief was torn,
To the city of Valencia the news was bourne.
To my Lord Cid the Champion, the message when it was brought,
For a full hour's space, he contemplated and he thought.
His hand he uplifted and gripped his beard again:

"To Christ be the glory, who over the whole earth does reign.
Those of Carrion cannot fail to keep my honour whole,
This beard has never was plucked by living soul.
To the Heirs of Carrion, no pleasure they will gain.
As for the ladies my daughters, I will marry them again.

Cid and all his men were upset, and very blue,
The heart and soul Alvar Fanez was torn in two.

Minaya with Pero Vermudoz straight away jumped on the horse,
And good Martin Antolinez in Burgos was on the course.
With two hundred horses, that to that end Cid set in array,
Most earnestly he commanded them to ride both night and day.
And to the city of Valencia his daughters they were to bring,
In reply to their Lord's commandment no one questioned a thing.
Swiftly they got on horseback, and rode both day and night,
Into Gormaz they entered, a strong city know for might.
Within the one night they stayed there, to Saint Stephen's the news flew,
That Minaya was coming, and to bring home his cousins too.
Saint Stephen's, home of the true and brave was the perception,
To Minaya and his men, the dwellers gave a noble reception.
And for a tribute to Minaya, brought to that night a good store,
Of cheer, but he desired not to accept it, but still thanked them therefor.

"Thanks, men of Saint Stephen's, all of you wise and brave,
For the honour you offer, for the things that you gave,
Cid the Champion gives his true thanks to you,
As I do here, may God give the payment your due."

And so they thanked him greatly, with him all were content,
Then swiftly to their lodging to rest, that night they all

went.
Minaya left to see them, and so went on his ways,
As he was coming Lady Sol and Elvira on him fixed their gaze:

"So heartily we thank you, as if our eyes on God were set,
And thank Him sincerely for it, since we are living yet.
In the days of ease after, in Valencia when we dwell,
The tale of our affliction, we will have the strength to tell.

Alvar Fanez and the ladies, let the tears flow from their eyes,
Pero Vermudoz observed them and sorely grieved likewise.

"Lady Sol and Elvira, do not be down-hearted still,
Since you are well and living and without any other ill.
You have lost a marriage, better matches we will make,
And may we soon behold the day when our vengeance we will take!"

So all that night they lay there keeping a merry cheer,
The next day in the morning they mounted the horses that were near,
The people of Saint Stephen's escorted them furthermore,
With every sort of comfort even to Riodamor.
There they left them, and got them in good stead to travel back,
Minaya and the ladies rode forward on the track.
They passed Alcoceva, and went through Gormaz that day,
They went over the river in the place called Vadorrey.
And in the town Berlanga, their lodging they had made,
The next day in the morning, onward went the cavalcade.
In a place called Medina, their shelter they had sought,
From Medina to Molina the next day the ladies were brought.

And there what the Moor Avengalvon saw pleased his eye,
He gave them a warm welcome and offered any supply.
For his love of Lord Cid, a dinner he gave them rich and great,
Then on to Valencia they then departed straight.
When to Cid the Champion, the news of this was sent,
Swiftly he got on horseback, and forward to greet them went.
As he rode he brandished weapons, very joyful was his face,
My Lord Cid came forward to his daughters to embrace.
And after he had kissed them, he smiled at the two:

"Here you are my daughters? God's will was to rescue you.
This marriage I accepted, daring not to say otherwise,
May the Creator grant it, who dwells up in the skies,
That you have better husbands, and hereafter how I long,
To see, the punishment of my sons of Carrion, for this wrong."

To kiss the hands of their father, the two bent down,
And under his protection they hastened and came into the town.
Their mother Lady Ximena, what a good cheer she made,
And he who was born in a good hour, neither delayed neither stayed,
But there to his comrades he spoke, make no mistake,
To King Alfonso of Castile the news of this they'll take.

"Where are you Muno Gustoz, servant who gives a fair report,
In a good time I cherished you and raised you in my court.
To King Alfonso in Castile the news you must take,
His hands with heart and spirit, kiss them for my sake,
I am known as his loyal servant, as my Lord he is known,

At the dishonour done to me by the heirs of Carrion,
The good King should be troubled in his soul and in his heart,
He gave them to wed my daughters, in this I had no part.
My girls they have deserted, with great dishonour thus,
They have put an insult by that action upon us.
Myself gave them no insult, but theirs is evident,
My possessions, which are mighty, off with them they went,
This and the other insult, which makes me ill content,
Bring them to meet with me, on a field or in parliament.
So that I may take my justice, on the heirs of Carrion,
Because in my heart the anguish exceedingly has grown."

Upon this, Muno Gustoz swiftly rode away,
To accompany him two horsemen followed as he led the way.
And with him were aides, that of the household type,
They departed from Valencia as fast as they could ride.
They gave themselves no rest either at night or at noon,
And King Don Alfonso found them in front of him soon.
Of Castile is he the ruler, of Galicia furthermore,
And likewise of Asturias, yes, to San Salvador.
As far as Santiago, paramount is he known,
The counts throughout Galicia, owe him for the sovereignty they own.

As soon as Muno Gustoz got down from horseback there,
Before the Saints he kneeled, and to God he made his prayer.
Where the court was in the palace, straightway his footsteps bent,
The two horsemen that served him, at their Lord's side went.
As soon as they had entered, among the royal train,

The King saw them and recognised Muno Gustoz again,
The King rose up and nobly he welcomed him well,
Before the King Alfonso on bended knees he fell.
At the King's feet, Muno Gustoz, kissed all:

"A favour, King, you of the sovereign kingdoms that they call,
The Champion, he kisses well your feet and hands,
You are his Lord; your servant at all times he stands.
Carrion's Heirs were given by you to wed Cid's daughters,
It was a glorious marriage, because it was your orders.
The honour we felt, is to you already known,
However, such disgrace was put on us by the Heirs of Carrion.
Fiercely they beat the daughters of Cid and what's more,
Naked, in great dishonour and from the beating they were sore,
In Corpes Wood unguarded they threw the girls away,
For any savage creatures and the forest-fowl for prey.
And now to Valencia his daughters are restored,
For this your hand he kisses as a servant to his Lord,
That you bring them to confront him, in person or in court,
He holds himself dishonoured, but you should be as well in thought,
And King, it should grieve you, and he prays for your advice how,
My Lord Cid may have justice on the Heirs of Carrion now."
The king was silent, pondering, and said on his part:

"The truth I will say to you, it grieves me to my heart,
So, Muno Gustoz, it was a true thing you said,
For Carrion's Heirs, his daughters I gave indeed to wed.
For good I did it, deeming that this was a good way,
But knowing this now the marriage would have never been

made today.
My Lord Cid and I myself, both grieved at heart are we,
I must help him to seek justice, as God our saviour be.
Though I would not at this season, but I must do it even so,
And now through all my Kingdom forward my men will go,
In Toledo city, in a court they will proclaim,
So that counts may come and noblemen that be of a lesser name.
To there the Heirs of Carrion, I will Summon furthermore,
And there they will give justice to Cid Champion my Lord.
Yet while I can prevent it, he will have no cause to mourn,
Go and tell the Champion, who in good hour was born,
That he may with his men, for these seven weeks prepare,
To come to Toledo, his wishes I grant him fair.
I will hold this meeting, since Cid to me is dear,
Greet them all for me fairly, let them be of joyful cheer.
For what happened, about the honour, they will have no lack."

With this, Muno Gustoz to my Lord Cid turned back.
Since he had declared that this charge on him should fall,
Alfonso the Castilian delayed it not at all.
To Leon and Santiago, he sent letters without fail,
And to the Galicians, and the men of Portingale.
News to those in Carrion, and in Castile they bring,
Of a Court held in Toledo, by the much honoured King.
And that there they must be gathered before seven weeks should end,
Whoever kept them hidden, no longer could pretend.
And with all men so determined throughout the breadth of his lands
Not to fail in the fulfilment, of the King's high commands.

Now are the Heirs of Carrion, were troubled by report,
That the King within Toledo was about to hold his court.

They feared Lord Cid Champion, will have a part within,
And so they sought advice, from their next of kin.
For the King, not to appear at the court they then prayed.

The King said: "I will not do it, and God will be my aid.
For my Lord Cid Champion, that place you will come to,
And you will give him justice for the complaint he makes of you.
Whoever refuses, or denies to attend my court,
Let him leave the realm, or you will be expelled in short.

And now the Heirs of Carrion saw that it must be done,
Since their very next of kin advised them, they could not run.
To ruin Cid, Count Garcia sought it evermore,
My Lord Cid's enemy shared in these matters like a guarantor.
This man gave advice to the Heirs of Carrion,
The time came: to the court the journey begun.
To there, among the many, the good King Alfonso did go,
With Count Don Henry, and Count Don Remond also.
The most respected, the most noble Emperor known,
Along came Count Don Froila and Count Don Birbon.
Out of his realm, came many of wise hearts and zeal,
All the best men were gathered from the kingdom of Castile.
And there with Crespo de Granon, Count Don Garcia came,
And he who ruled in Oca, Alvar Diaz was his name.
With Gonzalo Ansuorez, Ansuor Gonzalez stood,
Along with them was Pero of the Ansuorez brotherhood.
Diego and Fernando, were thinking of their last resort,
And with them a great group of men they brought to Court.
Upon Lord Cid, it was their intent to fall,
Around the place they gathered, from every side and every wall.

But he who in good hour was born, cared to arrive with ease,
Because he had delayed a little, the king was displeased,
My Lord Cid the Champion came on the fifth day,
He sent Alvar Fanez ahead of his array,
So he could kiss the King's hands, the Lord of his right,
So the King could know surely, that he would be there that night.
Now when the King had heard it, his heart was glad of course,
With company most mighty, the King leaped upon the horse,
And to he who was born in good hour, went to welcome there,
Cid came will all his men, exceedingly fair.
Such noble troops that follow a captain of such might!
When good King Don Alfonso, of Lord Cid caught sight,
My Lord Cid, the Champion, raised the sword,
So he could humble himself, and do honour to his Lord.

When the King saw he did not delay, "Saint Isidore on course!
This day you will Mount, Cid, upon the horse!
If not, my pleasure ends, let us greet on either part,
With heart and soul, what grieves you has hurt me to the heart.
God ordered that today in the court your honour will be defended."

My Lord Cid, the true Champion, to this said "Amen" and commended.
He kissed his hand and gave a fair greeting then:

"To God now thanks be given, that I see my Lord again.
To you I bow, and also to Count Don Remond I bow,

To Count Henry and to all men that are in my presence now.
God save our friends and foremost, Lord, may He cherish you,
My wife, Lady Ximena, the worthy Lady too,
Kiss your hands, my daughters, both do so as well,
So you may have pity for the ill thing that befell."

"Agreed! So God help me," answered the King.
Then onward to Toledo, the King returned with him.

Eager to cross the Tagus was my Lord Cid that night:

"A favour, King, the Creator, may he shield you with His might!
Oh Lord, are you ready to enter in the town?
In San Servan me and my men will settle down,
Because in the night, I rest those men of mine,
And I will keep my watch here, by the holy shrine.
I will come to town tomorrow at the breaking of the day,
And here I will eat my dinner, then to court will make my way."

The King gave his answer: "Surely, I am content."
Then the King Don Alfonso into Toledo went.
My Lord Cid Roy Diaz remained in San Servan,
To make candles and to set them on the shrine, his order ran.
To watch that sanctuary was the gladness of his heart,
As he prayed to the Creator and spoke to him, on his part.
Minaya, and as many others that were gathered of good fame,
Were in accord together when at length the morning came.

Morning prayers, and songs until the dawn had begun,
Before the sun had risen the mass was over and done.
With rich and timely offerings to the chapel they gave.

"Minaya Alvar Fanez, my strongest arm the brave.
You will keep me company and the Bishop Don Jerome,
Muno Gustoz and Pero Vermudoz all well know,
And Martin Antolinez from Burgos true and tried,
And with Alvar Salvadorez, Alvar Alvaroz on the side,
And Martin Munoz who was born in a season of good grace,
Likewise Felez Munoz a nephew of my race.
Mal Anda the wise, along with me shall go,
And the good Galant Garciaz of Aragon also.
With these knights, hundreds of the good men here ordain,
Let all men wear their armour, to assist and sustain,

Put chains around the neck, that white as sunlight shine,
And over the white chains, coats of the same kind,
Let them lace their armour tight, don't let the arms be seen,
What they carry beneath their coats, swords both sweet and clean.
To the court in such fashion to enter am I eager,
It's my right to demand an answer, from both of them, or either.
If there, the Heirs of Carrion seek to dishonour me,
I will not fear them, even if a hundred strong they be."

To him all gave their answer: "Lord, your will is our desire,"
Even as he was commanding, they organised their attire.

He who was born in happy hour, would accept no more delay,
Around his legs the trousers of fair cloth he threw on

straight away,
And shoes adorned most richly, placed upon his feet was done;
He donned a shirt of linen, fine and as white as the sun,
The sleeves were laced, moreover, with gold and silver braid,
The cuff fit close to the wrist, just as he asked them to be made.
Overall a silk coat, of the most fair white he threw,
The threads of gold shone brightly that were woven through and through.
A red fur gown, and gold-belt he placed over the coat of his,
That gown he always wore, the great champion, Lord Cid.
He had the finest linen cap upon his hair,
With golden thread, moreover, fashioned with due care.
So the locks of the Champion, might not be disarrayed,
And with his beard so thick, my Lord Cid had it in a braid.
All this he did desiring to be ready when he got close,
Over his attire, a coat of mighty worth he throws.
From San Servan onward he spurred his horse with pace,
Cid swiftly departed to that judgment-place.
Then without delay, he descended from his horse,
And prudently he entered the palace with his force.

He went in, his hundred men round on every side,
When all had seen him enter, they observed him with pride.
Then the good King Alfonso on his feet did rise,
And so did Count Don Henry, and Count Don Remond likewise.
And all arose, the others of the court, you may know,
To him who in good hour was born, a great honor they did show.

One man there, did not arise: Crespo de Granon,
And neither any of the party, of the Heirs of Carrion.

The King took Lord Cid's hand: "Come and sit with me,
On the bench here beside me, you are a gift to me.
You are our better, though there be an offence here to note."

Then he who won Valencia out of gratitude spoke:
"Sit like a king and master on your bench, as it is yours;
In this place I will not delay here with the men indoors."

For what my Lord Cid had said the King's was glad and did not speak,
On a bench well made, Cid then took his seat,
The hundred men that guard him, sat round him there,
And all men in the Court, upon my Lord Cid did stare,
And at the long beard he wore that was braided with a cord,
He seemed by his apparel to be a splendid Lord.
Out of shame, the Heirs of Carrion, his gaze they could not meet.

The good King Don Alfonso then rose to his feet:
"Hear me gentlemen, so God sustains your hands,
Only two courts before, I have held in the space of all my lands.
On in Burgos, in Carrion the next I did array,
The third here in Toledo I have come to hold today,
For Cid's love, whose good birth is well known,
So he may have justice on the Heirs of Carrion.
Let all men know they did him a bitter insult,
The Counts Remond and Henry, have yet to place the fault,
And all you counts, moreover, in the feud who bear no part.
In your minds turn it over, as you are wise of heart.
See that you render justice, I encourage in the least,

On one side and the other let us keep the peace,
Who breaks our peace, I swear, by Saint Isidore,
Will be banished from my Kingdom, and have my favour nevermore.
His side I will maintain, whose cause is right and fair,
Therefore let Cid Champion give his account and declare.
Then we will hear what Carrion's Heirs in answer will depose."

My Lord Cid kissed the King's hand, then to his feet he rose:
"My sovereign and my master great thanks I give to you,
That this court you have summoned out of a pure love so true,
Against the Heirs of Carrion, this the matter that I claim,
They cast away my daughters, and in this I had no blame.
As you gave them in marriage, so what should be done today.
You know well, from Valencia when they took my girls away,
I loved with heart and spirit the Heirs of Carrion,
And the two swords I gave them, Colada and Tizon,
I won them in such manner, as a good knight I became,
That they might do you service and do honour to their name.
When in the Wood of Corpes, they left my girls alone,
They lost my love forever, as they made their hate for me known.
Since they are no longer my sons-in-law, let them give me either sword."

"All of the claim is righteous," the judges gave accord.

Then Count Don Garcia said: " Of this, let us debate."

To hold a discussion among them, the Heirs of Carrion went straight,
And all their following with them and the people of their name.
And swiftly they debated, and to their resolve they came:

"A great favour for us, Cid Champion did do,
Since for his girls' dishonor, no damage does he sue.
With King Don Alfonso, we will soon be at one,
The swords, let us give him, and then the suit is done.
They will hold the court no longer, when he has them once again,
From us no further justice for Lord Cid Champion."

That being over, to the court they took the swords.

"Your favour, King Alfonso, and all you other Lords,
We cannot deny it, he gave them as he said,
And since we now return them, may his desires be met,
Into his hand to give them, in your presence for all to see."

Then they brought forth Colada and Tizon which shone faultlessly.
Straight away they gave them over to the King's sovereign's hands,
The whole court shone so glorious, when the light hit the stands.
The handle and blades, were all of massy gold,
To the true men of the court, it was a marvel to behold.

The King my Lord Cid summoned, to him the swords he gave.
His sovereign's hands he kissed, as he received each blade.
To the bench where he had risen, he turned back again,
And in his hands he held them, as he looked toward his

men.
Counterfeits they could not give him, he knew the two aright,
And his heart laughed within him, he was filled with all delight.

"Now on my beard that no one ever plucked, for Heaven's Sake,
For Lady Sol and Lady Elvira high vengeance I will take."

To his nephew Pero he called out loud, "for the wrong."
And stretching forth his hand, he gave him Tizon.

"Take it nephew, the sword's master now is of better renown."

To good Martin Antolinez the man of Burgos town,
Stretching forth his hand, Colada, into his care he gave,

"You Martin Antolinez, the brave,
Take Colada that I captured from a true knight without fail,
From he of Barcelona, from Remond Berenguel.
So you may guard it rightly, therefore to you, it I give,
I know if anything happens, if on occasion I cease to live,

Great fame and estimation with the sword you will attain."

He kissed Lord Cid's hands and he took the sword again.

My Lord Cid the Champion then rose to say another thing:

"Now thanks to the Creator and to my Lord the King.
With the swords Colada and Tizon I am content indeed,
But I have another issue against the Carrion Heirs to plead.
When with them from Valencia my daughters they took the

two,
Three thousand coins of silver and gold I gave them too.
When I did this, the winning end is all they saw,
Let them restore, the treasure, they are not my sons-in-law."

What a complaint they made, the Carrion's Heirs were angered so,
To them Count Don Remond said: "Give your answer, 'Yes' or 'No!',
And then the Heirs of Carrion, made their answer plain:

"To Cid Champion we gave his swords again,
So he would demand nothing further, so his suit should be closed thereby."

Then straight away Count Don Remond said to all in reply:

"This we say, with the pleasure of the Sovereign if it stands,
That you should not give satisfaction to what Cid demands."

The good King said: "The amount with my acceptance it does meet."
And now Cid Champion had arisen to his feet:

"Those goods I gave you, will you give them to me anew,
Or render an account?" Then Carrion's Heirs withdrew.

To give back the greatness of that treasure, neither could consent,
As the two Heirs of Carrion, the whole of it had spent.
They returned with their decision, and made their plea as thus:

"The Captor of Valencia, presses sore on us.

Since he desires for his possessions, which on his hand he laid,
From our estates in Carrion the money will be paid."

And then the judges spoke since the debt the Heirs avowed:

"If it's Cid's desire, it is not disallowed.
So we ordain, as the issue it does sort,
That you repay it to him, in the presence of the court."

King Alfonso spoke, when their words were at an end:

"The secret of this law we wholly comprehend,
That justice is demanded by Lord Cid,
Now those three thousand coins, I have in hand to give;
They were given to me by the Heirs of Carrion before.
Since they impoverished, I will give them back and more,
To Cid born in a fair hour, let them pay the money back.
To pay their debt, that money I will not let them lack."

As for Fernando Gonzalez, what he has to say you will now hear:

"We have in our possession no minted goods or gear."

To him then the Count Don Remond answered to this intent:

"All of the gold and silver, the pair of you have spent.
Before the King Alfonso, our verdict we proclaim,
That you pay it in goods to the Champion, and let him accept the same."

Now the Heirs of Carrion saw what their course is,
Seeing led away their donkeys and many swift horses,

Moreover, and many rings with well-placed jade,
And every sort of armour, and many swords of fine blade.
My Lord Cid accepted all, as the court assessed,
Beyond the coins of gold, which Alfonso possessed,
To him who was born in good hour, the Heirs have paid the price,
Others' goods they borrowed, as their own would not suffice.
Men would take them as fools, from that suit when the pair leave.
And when taking all of those great possessions my Lord Cid was pleased.

The men kept all that treasure, and they will guard it well,
When it was done, the thinking of other things then fell:

"Lord King, for love of me, a further favour yet,
Out of my complaints the main one, I cannot forget.
Let the whole court hear me now, and have pity on my woe:
As these Heirs of Carrion, the pair have shamed me so,
Do not allow them to leave unchallenged, so they may get away,
In what way have I offended you, what do you Heirs of Carrion say,
In what fashion whatsoever, in earnest or in sport,
Let me make amends, according to the judgment of the court.
Why did you tear in to pieces the fabric of my heart?
From Valencia you left with honour, when it was time to depart,
I gave to you my daughters, and besides great wealth and gear,
What do you say, you dogs and traitors, why did you not hold them dear?
Why take them from Valencia? Which was theirs to inherit.

And with wrath and anger, you beat the ladies without any merit.
Alone in Corpes Forest you threw the pair away,
To the savage creatures in the wood to be their prey.
In all you did to them, your vileness you show,
Let the Court judge; will I get satisfaction, or a no?"

And then, Count Don Garcia rose up again:

"Let us now have your decision, best of all the kings of Spain,
About what Cid announced, who is well versed in the affairs,
He let it out so mighty, it is a long beard he wears,
But this sounds frightening and fear is a sorry case,
But as for them of Carrion, they are a proud race,
His daughters were taken as lovers, but did they love them, no,
Themselves as lawful wives those ladies would not show.
When they cast them off, perhaps this was befit.
All things he says moreover we value not a bit."

Upon this, the Champion gripped his beard:

"To God who rules all of Heaven the almighty shall be cheered.
Since tenderly I kept it, my beard has grown so long,
Count, say what is the reason, that you do my beard this wrong.
Since its first growth, it has been so gently reared,
No man or woman born, has ever plucked this beard.
But once in Cabra Castle, I did, oh Count to yours,
That one time in Cabra, I held your beard like a Moors.
I did not pluck or pick it, in no way it could ever get,
Nor is it grown as much as mine, even with the part I did

tear.
Here hidden in my wallet is a piece of it I bear."

Now Fernando Gonzalez rose to his feet with pride,
What he said, you will now hear, so loud he cried:

"Cid, do you now give up the suit which you have made,
As the whole of your possessions into your hands is paid.
See that you do not make greater, the feud between you and us,
As two Counts of Carrion by lineage we are thus.
Of kings' and emperors' daughters, we are fit to win the hands,
To wed the girls of little chiefs, is not where our lineage stands.
When your daughters were abandoned, we did what was right,
Not worse, but better, we are then within our own sight."

To Pero Vermudoz, Roy Diaz my Lord Cid looked now:

"Speak good Pero, you are a silent, how?
The ladies are my daughters, it is your cousins that they beat,
Into your teeth they threw it, with such a thing they speak.
You will not do this battle, if it is I that talks,
And Pero Vermudoz began the story, after he gathered up his thoughts.
No words he speaks clearly, as he is a tongue twisted man,
Nevertheless, no rest he gave them, when he finally began:

"For you Cid I tell it, as your customs be,
That in Court, Pero, never have you ever called me.
And really you know that I can do no more,
As for what I must accomplish, there will be no lack

therefore.
The thing you have said Fernando, what a lie.
Through the Champion your glory had risen ever more high.
I can relate a little, but not to every trick and sleight,
Do you remember in high Valencia, that time we fought the fight?
You were, for the true Champion, the first pray,
And there was a Moor you saw, who you went forth to slay.
And when he came closer, before him, didn't you run?
If I had not aided you, surely you would have been done.
But I rushed on to save you, and with the Moor very close,
I made that Moor run backward and struck some mighty blows.
To you I gave his horse, and kept the thing concealed,
Until this day your cowardice I never have revealed.
Before Cid and all men, your own praises, didn't you sing?
How you killed the Morisco, and did a gallant thing.
And they believed it from you, knowing not the truth at all,
Your faces might be handsome, but your courage is so small.
A tongue without hands, the manhood to speak where did you get it from?
What do you say Fernando, are these words the truth or wrong?
That matter of the lion in Valencia, in memory do you keep?
When he burst his bonds, while Cid lay asleep?
Fernando, then what did you do? When in your terror, was overcome,
Didn't you thrust yourself behind the bench of Cid Champion.
Did you hide Fernando, that's why cheap today your worth is found,
But to guard our Lord and master, his bench we gathered

round,
Until he who won Valencia, out of his sleep was awake,
He rose up from the bed, toward the lion, didn't he make?
His head the lion bended, for Cid the beast stopped to wait,
By the neck he let himself be taken, and in the cage he threw him straight.
When the Champion returned, he looked at his men where they stand,
He asked about his sons-in-law, but neither were found at hand.
You wicked man and traitor, your character is so plain,
In fight before Alfonso, the same I will maintain,
For Lady Sol and Lady Elvira, for Cid's daughters' sake,
You threw away the ladies, for your honour, which is cheap to make.
You are men to all in appearance, tender women are those two,
Yet in every way whatever they are worthier than you.
If, when we have the combat, God likes it from afar,
You will confess it, like the traitor that you are.
Whatever I have said then will be known as true."

And this was the end of speech between the two.

What Diego Gonzalez replied, you will now hear:

"We are Counts by lineage of blood of the most clear.
Such marriages in no way we would usually undertake,
With my Lord Cid Don Rodrigo, the alliance we did make.
We do not yet repent, that we said to his daughters 'bye',
And so long as life endures, may they sigh and sigh.
A sore reproach on them what we did will still remain.
But with utmost valour in a fight I will maintain,
When we cast away the women we made our honour good."

Then Martin Antolinez to his feet he stood:

"You fool, keep your silence. Mouth that the truth knows not!
The matter of the lion have you so soon forgot?
Out through the door you fled, lurking in the court outside,

Behind the wine-press timber, in that hour, hiding inside,
Your coat was no longer on you to see,
In fight I will maintain it, no other way it can be.
Since Lord Cid daughters, into such a dilemma you threw,
They are in every fashion far worthier than you.
At the end of combat, your own mouth will open the jar,
That lies are all you speak, and a traitor you are."

Between those two the meeting had come to an end.

Now Ansuor Gonzalez came into the palace then,
With a white cloak on him, and his tunic trailing behind,
His face was a bit messy, as lately he had dined.
In what he had to say, little discretion he did show:

"Listen you noble gentlemen, this is ever such a woe,
With Vivar's Lord Cid, such honour, who would have thought to find?
On the river's water, let his millstones grind,
And take his toll, would any man have thought,
That with the Heirs of Carrion, alliances he sought?"

Muno Gustoz rose to his feet forthright:

"You fool, stay silent! You are a wicked traitor right!
Before you say your prayers you go to dine of course,
Whoever's in peace, you kiss and sicken them with that belch yours.

Whether to a friend or master you speak rubbish too,
False to all, and falsest to God, who made you.
Never in your friendship, or even from a far,
Will I be yours, I will make you say, what I say you are."

King Alfonso said: "Let the suit now lie.
Who have challenged each other should battle, so help me the Most High. "

Soon as the suit was finished, to the court, two horsemen came,
Inigo Ximenez and Ojarra was the name,
Navarra's Heir, a suitor, was one,
The other was a suitor, the Heir of Aragon.
And there they both together kissed Alfonso's hand,
Cid Champion's daughters in marriage they demand,
Of the realms Navarre and Aragon, the lady-queens to be,
May he send them with his blessing and with all courtesy.
The whole court listened, and stillness fell over them,
On his feet he rose, straight away, my Lord Cid Champion:

"A favour, Oh King Alfonso, my Lord on your part,
For this to the Creator very thankful is my heart,
Since both Navarre and Aragon have made a request so high,
You gave my daughters to wed before, you know it was not I.
Here then are my daughters, both are in your hand,
With them I will do nothing, except at your command."

The King rose up, to break the silence, his word he then gave:

"I beg it of you, Champion, the true Cid and the brave,
That here you yield in agreement. I will grant the thing this

day,
And it will be consented in this court straight away,
Because it will grow your glory, your honour, and your lands."

Now is Cid arose and kissed Alfonso's hands:

"To whatever pleases you, I give consent, my Lord."

Then the King said: "God grant you an excellent reward!
Inigo Ximenez and Ojarra, to you two,
I yield my full permission for this marriage to you,
That Lady Sol and Lady Elvira, who Cid's daughters are,
Wed, one the Heir of Aragon, and the other of Navarre.
May he yield his girls with blessings in an honourable way."

Then Inigo Jimenez and Ojarra, stood and made their way,
To the hands of Don Alfonso, to kiss them again,
Then the hands of Cid, they kissed the pair of them.
And there their faith they pledged and solemn oaths they swore,
That they would fulfil entirely what they promised and yet more.
Because of this, many in the court were exceedingly glad;
But the two Heirs of Carrion, in this no joy they had.

Minaya Alvar Fanez jumped to his feet fast:

"From my King and Master, a favour that I ask,
And let it not be detrimental to Cid,
I have throughout this meeting kept my peace under a lid,
But now to say somewhat, on my own part, eager am I."
The King said: "Now all my spirit, from this is well pleased

by.
Speak Minaya, say what to your heart is dear."

"You in the court, I beg you, to my words lend an ear.
Against Carrion's Heirs, charges I most mightily bring,
I gave to them my cousins by Alfonso's hand, the King.
With blessings and with honour they took them in their care,
Then Cid Champion gave them the most rich possessions there.
They cast away those ladies, and forgot their oath,
As wicked men and traitors, I am challenging you both.
From the great sons of Gomez, your lineage comes down,
From who many counts have come, of valour and renown,
But this day, certainly their cunning we can learn,
For this to the Creator, thanks I do return,
Those of Navarre and Aragon, the Heirs, in marriage pursue,
Lady Sol and Elvira, that are my cousins too.
Formerly for true wives you had them, who now their hands will kiss,
And call them their Lady, really it is you who took a miss.
Praise to our God in Heaven and our Lord the King in one,
This greatly grows the honour of Cid the Champion.
In every way whatsoever, you are exactly as say,
Is there any in our presence, who think another way?
I am Alvar Fanez, who will fight against the most of might!"

And then Gomez Pelaez stood upright:

"Say what you like Minaya, but as you speak so free,
There are men here in the court, that think oppositely.
Thinking otherwise, and would ruin him indeed,
If it be by chance, God's pleasure, that our dispute we

should proceed,
Then you will see whether right or wrong you were."

The King said: "The suit is over, no other charges I prefer.
Tomorrow is the combat, at the rising of the sun
The those who challenged the others, in the court it will be done."

The Heirs of Carrion then spoke presently:

"Lord King, tomorrow it cannot be,
We have given to the Champion our arms and horses indeed,
First to our land of Carrion, to go we have a need."

The King then spoke to the Champion again:
"Where would you like this combat to be undertaken."

"My Lord, I will not do it," Lord Cid said highly,
"More than the lands of Carrion, Valencia likes me."

To him the King gave his answer: "That's without a doubt,
Give to me your knights, all duly armed about.
Let them go in my keeping, their safety I assure,
As a Lord to a good servant, I'll make the path secure.
So they take no harm, from any count or lower man,
Now here in the court, a term for them I plan,
That in the fields of Carrion at the end of three weeks' space,
There duly in my presence the combat will take place.
Who at this set time, does not come, his suit is lost thereby,
From that time he is vanquished, as a traitor let him fly."

The two heirs of Carrion, after the order, both took a stand.
And upon this my Lord Cid kissed Alfonso's hand.

"Into your hand they are delivered, my knights to do,
Your will my King and Master, I entrust them to you.
They are ready now, their duty to the full and undertake.
With honour to Valencia send them to me for God's sake."

"Let it be God's desire," the King said.

Cid the Champion took off his helmet from his head,
Likewise the cap of linen as white as the sun,
He freed his beard, the cord around it he now undone.
Those in the court around him, in full could not gaze,
To the Counts Remond and Henry forward he went his way.
And them closely he embraced, and offered all they require,
To take possessions from him, all that they desire.
These two, and many others who were people of good will,
He earnestly requested to take until their fill.
Some took his gifts, but others would not accept a thing,
The two hundred coins he gave again, once more to the King.
Whatever was his pleasure, he has taken from the rest:

"King, for love of the Creator, one more thing that I request.
Lord, with your will I kiss your hand, since these deeds are done,
I would eagerly go to Valencia which with great pain I won."

Then Cid commanded to give horses to the Heirs of Navarre and Aragon,
For their men, and whatever else they asked for it was done.
Then he sent them forward, King Don Alfonso with all his men,

Who got on horseback in order for Cid to ride with them.
When they came to Zocodover, Cid being on Bavieca,

The King said to him: "In faith, Don Rodrigo, you could do better,
To make that charger faster, of which I have heard the most fair report."

Cid smiled and said: "Lord, many gentle and simple men in your court,
Who would gladly do such a thing, ask one to push their horse."

The King replied to him: "Cid, with your answer, I am pleased of course,
Nevertheless I desire you, for the love you have for me,
To put that horse through his best paces, as fast as he can be."

Cid then heeled the charger and made him gallop fast,
So fast that all were astonished in the end he ran at last.
The King with his hand uplifted, signed the cross upon his face,
By San lsidoro of Leon, I swear it by his grace
There is no nobleman so mighty, in this country of ours."

My Lord Cid came back to the King, after he had witnessed his powers,
And before his Lord Alfonso, he kneeled and kissed his hand.

"To push Bavieca, you gave me your command.
Today no Moor or Christian has a horse so strong and swift,
Lord, to you I give him, say you will accept the gift."

The King then said: "This would give me no pleasure indeed,
If I took him, then less glorious the master would be of that amazing steed.
But a horse like this, is suited to a man like you, you see,
Swift to chase the Moors, routed in the battle, when they flee.
Whoever takes that war-horse from you, God will not support again,
Because by you and by the charger a great honour we attain."
Then their leave they took, he left the Court forthright,
The Champion most wisely advised all who were to fight:

"Martin Antolinez! Pero Vermudoz, you too,
Likewise Muno Gustoz my tried man and true.
Be resolute in combat like the gentlemen you be,
See that good news of you, in Valencia finds me."

Martin Antolinez said: "Oh Lord, give us your advice, how?
As we must bear the burden that we have accepted now.
You will hear nothing of us vanquished, but gladly of the killed."

He who was born in a happy hour, from this was glad and was filled.
From all his leave he took, now all his friends are known,
My Lord Cid went to Valencia, and the King to Carrion.

But now the three weeks' space of the term was past and done,
At the time appointed, they who serve the Champion,
The debt to their Lord laid on them, they were very eager to repay,

In safe-keeping of Alfonso, King of Leon, they had made their way.

There, for the Heirs of Carrion for two days they stayed,
With horses and armour, came the Heirs well arrayed.
And in the distance from them, all their men had said,
On the Champion's men, in secret they might attack and leave them dead,
Killing them in the meadows, without their lords consent,
They did not undertake it, although that had the foul intent,
Because of Alfonso of Leon, they stood in mighty dread,
So they watched over their arms that night, and prayers to God they said.
At last the night passed over, and then broke the dawn,
Many worthy noblemen to that place had drawn,
To observe that combat, therefore they were there to visit,
Moreover King Alfonso above all men was of good spirit.
Since he desired justice and that no wrong should be done,
The men of the good Champion, got their armour on.
All three were in agreement as one Lord's men they stay tight,
The Heirs of Carrion elsewhere, armed themselves for the fight.
The Count Garci Ordonez sat with them, to advise them there.
What they should say to the King Alfonso and what they should declare,
That neither Colada or Tizon in battle should have a share,
That in fight they could not wield them, as it would be unfair.
That the swords were given over, they deemed it to be ill,
So to the King they said it, but he would not do their will.

"When we held the court, no sword exception did you make,
If you have good weapons, your fortune they will make.

For them who serve the Champion the swords they choose will do,
Now Carrion's Heirs, to the battle ground you two!
If you are worthy, you should be able to say you have won,
For the Champion, his men will leave nothing undone.
If you are victorious, then great will be your fame,
But if you are vanquished, credit to us no blame.
You know you sought it." Carrion's Heirs were filled with grief each one,
And greatly they repented the thing that they had done.
To have it undone, they would have paid any fee.

The men of the Champion, were fully armed, all three.

Now King Alfonso came forth before the battle had begun,
Then he said to the men, that served the Champion:

"We kiss the hands as servants of our Lord and master, may,
He between our party and their party, give judgement on this day.
For our support of justice, no evil will stand.

Carrion's Heirs, then gathered in a band.

"We do not know, what in secret they intend,
But our Lord in your hand left us our safety to defend.
For the love of the Creator, we maintain just on our part."

The King then said in answer: "With all my soul and all my heart."

They brought for them the chargers of splendid strength and speed.
They signed the cross on the saddles, they leaped upon the steed.
The buckles embossed, around their necks were cast,
And with pointed lances, in their hands they gripped them fast.
Each lance for each man of the three, its own banner to bear,
And many worthy men had gathered round them there.
To the field within the boundaries, accordingly they went,
The three men of the Champion, were all of one intent.
That mightily his enemy to destroy each one should ride,
And then the saw the Heirs of Carrion on the other side.

With stores of men, as many of their kin were with the two,
The King has given them judges for justice and nothing else to do.
That yes or no, they were not to make any move,
To them, where in the field they were, King Alfonso went to.
"Listen you Heirs of Carrion to these things to you I say:
In Toledo you contrived it, but you did not wish this fray.
From my Lord Cid the Champion I brought these knights, all three,
To Carrion's land, that under my safe-conduct they might be.
This is justice, do not turn to evil, even in intent,
Whoever so desires evil, with force I will prevent.
After such a thing throughout my kingdom, he will surely moan."

How sad and pessimistic were the Heirs of Carrion!

Now the King with the judges had marked the boundaries out,
They cleared all the meadow of the people roundabout.
And to the men the boundaries, they have clearly shown,
Whoever goes beyond them, should be considered overthrown.
The people that were gathered round, now all the space left clear,
To approach they were forbidden, or they will face the spear.
Against the sun no man was stationed, but each was given his place.
Forward, between them came the judges, and the foes were face to face.
Lord Cid's men, toward the Heirs of Carrion went,
And Carrion's Heirs against them, went with the same intent.
The eye of every man, fixed on his man in sight,
Before their horses with their hands the shields gripped tight.
The lances with the banners, now they have pointed low,
And each ducked his head over the saddlebow.
And with their heels they kicked, the battle-chargers so they,
As if the earth had shaken, quickly sprang away.
The glance of every man fixed on his man in sight,
Two against two together, now joined in the fight.

Those who stood round for certain, thought the dead would soon fall,
Pero Vermudoz, the challenge, delivered first of all,
Against Fernando Gonzalez there, face to face he sped,

They struck each other's shields without ending any dread.
Fernando Gonzalez pierced Don Pero's target through,
But his lance-shaft in two places, shattered it in two.
To the flesh it did not go, as it barely touched the steel,
Pero Vermudoz sat firmly, and did not make a squeal.
For every stroke that was dealt him, a strike back he gave,
He broke Fernando's shield, the shield now he did crave.
He drove through the guard and armour, all through the man's gear,
Straight to the heart, into the chest he thrust the battle-spear.
Three layers of armour Fernando had, and the third was of avail,
Two were burst through, yet third stopped the nail.
Fernando's shirt and coat, with the unpierced iron mesh,
A hair away, by Pero Vermudoz were thrust into the flesh.
And from his mouth straight away a stream of blood began to spout,
His stirrups were broken, not one of them had held out.
Over the tail of the horse, he hurled to the ground,
He had got his death stroke, thought all the folk around.
He left the war-spear in him, placed his hand upon his sword,
When Fernando Gonzalez saw it, he knew Tizon was coming forward.

He shouted, "I am vanquished," the blows I cannot bear,
Pero Vermudoz, the judges pronounced the winner and then left him there.

With Diego Gonzalez, Don Martin came close,
With spears, they broke the lances so furious were the blows.
Martin Antolinez on his sword, his hand he laid,
The whole field shone, so brilliant and flawless was the

blade.
He struck a blow, sideways it caught him fair and right,
Aside the upper helmet, what a stroke to strike.

It smashed the helmet laces, through the iron-hood it went,
Through the cover, hard slashing and made the helmet bent,
And scraped the hair upon his face, clear to the flesh it sped,
Half the helmet fell to the ground, the other half crowned his head.
When the glorious Colada, such a war-stroke had let drive,
Diego Gonzalez knew it well, that he could not escape alive.
He turned the charger's rein, and right around he wheeled,
A blade in his hand he carried, that he did not seek to wield.
Martin Antolinez, welcomed the sword he got,
With the blow Martin struck him, his name he almost forgot.
From that, that Heir of Carrion, a mighty yell he gave:

"Help me, Oh God most glorious, defend me from that knave."
Wheeling his horse, in terror he fled before the blade.
The horse took him past the boundary, on the field Don Martin stayed.

Then the King said: "Now come to me you two,
Such deeds you have accomplished, that has won this fight for you."

The true words he had spoken, every judge deemed well.
The two had won, but about Muno Gustoz let us tell,
How with Ansuor Gonzalez, an account of himself he drew,
Against each other's shields the mighty strokes they threw.
Ansuor Gonzalez, was a gallant man of might,

Against Don Muno Gustoz, on the shield he gave a strike.
And piercing through the shied, right through the breastplate broke,
Slack went the lance, his body was unwounded by the stroke.
That blow struck Nuno Gustoz, but he let it fly.
Through the breastplate in the middle, the armour was burst thereby.
Away he could not ward it, through his breastplate it did dart,
Through one side it was driven, though not into his heart.
At the side of his body, he thrust the sharp spear,
On the far side he thrust it, however it was fully clear.
He held it and gave one pull, out of the saddle that knight he threw,
Down to the earth he cast him, when out the lance he drew.
The shaft, the lance and spear, all crimson they came out,
All thought that he was wounded, to his death without a doubt.
The lance he recovered, his foe he stood above,
He said to Gonzalo Ansuorez: "I strike for God my love.
Now the combat is won, because this game is done."

"We have heard defeat conceded," said the judges, everyone.

The good King Don Alfonso, asked them to clear the field straight away,
Because he himself took the armour, upon it that lay.
In honour all departed, who serve Cid and furthermore,
Glory be to the Creator, they have conquered in the war.
Throughout the lands of Carrion, sorrow was at a height,
The King my Lord, sent Cid's men away that night,
And ensured, they should not be frightened or ambushed on the way,

Like men of prudent spirit, they journeyed night and day.
Finally in Valencia with Cid the Champion they stand,
On Carrion's Heirs the jokers, the three have stamped the brand,
And delivered all to the Lord Cid said to get done,
On that account, very merry, was Cid Champion.
Upon the heirs of Carrion, came such a shame, who could,
Take a noble lady and then leave her in the wood?
May karma come around to them, or worse fortune let them find,
The dealings of Carrion's Heirs, let us leave behind.
Because any good associated to them, now no longer did,
Let us mention now, the grand man, Lord Cid,
And the great rejoice, through Valencia the town,
Because the Champion's men had won such great renown.
Their Lord Roy Diaz said, who had waited and been patient:

"Thanks to the King of Heaven, revenge has been taken.
Now may they hold in their Carrion lands, shame never to be wiped away.
I will wed my daughters in great honour, let it upset whomever it may."

Those of Navarre and Aragon, were eager for their treat,
And with Alfonso of Leon's consent, soon they will meet.
Lady Sol and Lady Elvira in due course wedded they are,
Great were their former matches, but these are better by far.
He gave with greater honour, than before, the two to be wed,
He who was born in a happy hour, still his glory spreads,
Since over Navarre and Aragon as queens his daughters reign,
Today are they are relatives to the Kings of Spain.
From him came all that honour, who in good hour had his

birth,
Cid who ruled Valencia, has departed from the earth,
On the seventh Sunday after Easter, may Christ's Mercy to him extend,
To us all, just men or sinners, may He always stand our friend.

END

For more adapted classics by James Harris please visit:

Http://ViewAuthor.at/JamesHarris